A powerful book of love and hope. *Fighting for David* dispels the myth that the quality of life determines its value. Mrs. Nunley has poignantly shown us the beauty of the severely disabled as only a loving mother could. As someone who fought for Terri Schiavo, I commend Mrs. Nunley for her success in helping her son David. This book will challenge your heart to appreciate life as a precious gift from God.

DAVID GIBBS III
Attorney for Terri Shiavo's parents, Bob and Mary Schindler

Any family that has been through something similar, as ours has, will recognize everything Leone describes—and most of us will share her determination to help this loved one recover his life and personality and purpose, no matter what dire predictions the doctors make. *Fighting for David* is a wonderful account of how God works with believing people through any crisis, not always with instantaneous miracles, but with a continuing, strengthening and encouraging Presence.

PAT BOONE
Entertainer and recording artist

This is one of the most incredible books I have ever read. It is a deeply moving story of heartache and courage, of brokenness and beauty, of lost dreams and new dreams. When I came to the last page, I didn't want the story to end—and in many ways it hasn't. *Fighting for David* has encouraged my heart, and I believe it will profoundly impact the life of every person who reads it.

ALICE GRAY
Author of *Treasures for Women Who Hope* and *Stories for the Heart*

Fighting for David

LEONE NUNLEY
WITH DEAN MERRILL

TYNDALE HOUSE PUBLISHERS, INC.
CAROL STREAM, ILLINOIS

Visit Tyndale's exciting Web site at www.tyndale.com

TYNDALE and Tyndale's quill logo are registered trademarks of Tyndale House Publishers, Inc.

Fighting for David

Designed by Beth Sparkman

Edited by Kimberly Bates Miller

Published in association with the Van Diest Literary Agency

Published in association with the literary agency of Mark Sweeney & Associates, Bonita Springs, Florida 34135

Library of Congress Cataloging-in-Publication Data

Nunley, Leone.
    Fighting for David: a true story of stubborn love, faith, and hope beyond reason / Leone Nunley with Dean Merrill.
    p. cm.
    Includes bibliographical references (p.   ).
    ISBN-13: 978-1-4143-0974-3 (sc)
    ISBN-10: 1-4143-0974-0 (sc)
    1. McRae, David, 1968—Health.   2. Brain damage—Patients—United States—Biography. 3. Brain damage—Patients—United States—Family relationships   4. Brain damage—Religious aspects—Christianity.
I. Merrill, Dean.   II. Title.
RC387.5.N86M37 2006
617.4¢81044092—dc22   2005031015

Printed in the United States of America

12   11   10   09   08   07   06
7   6   5   4   3   2   1

THANKS MOM, I.
I DVE YOU.
DAVID

CONTENTS

Foreword
by David B. Fletcher, PhD

Over a decade ago, two similar tragedies began to unfold on opposite sides of the United States. One of them, which began in 1990, became internationally known, while the other, which started a year earlier, is detailed in this book. Both of the victims of these tragedies fell into what doctors called a persistent vegetative state, and both of their families were told that there was no hope for recovery. The outcomes, however, were dramatically different—one became a story of defeat, the other one of hope.

In the spring of 2005, Americans became aware of a fifteen-year struggle that had raged over the life of Mrs. Terri Schiavo, a young woman who had collapsed after her heart stopped beating and she was left unconscious. Terri was said to be in a persistent vegetative state, which means that she was wakeful but unaware, unable to feel pleasure or pain, to feel emotions, to interact, or to respond. Not all physicians involved in the case concurred with this diagnosis, however. With round-the-clock coverage of the debacle on the cable news outlets, everyone came to know about this woman, her husband, and her parents. Terri's husband, Michael Schiavo, petitioned the court in 1998 to discontinue the feeding and hydration that kept her alive, while her parents, Bob and Mary Schindler, fought to keep the feeding going and to keep her alive.

The details of the drama are familiar to most people, from the court battles, to the involvement of Florida governor Jeb Bush and his brother President George W. Bush, to the attempts by Congress to intervene. Americans continue to be deeply divided over the case. Many, including a great number of Christians, strongly supported maintaining Terri's life and applauded government steps to intervene. However, this group was in the minority, as polls showed that most Americans approved of the decision to let her die and resented Congress for getting involved. In fact, 59 percent of Americans agreed "strongly" or "somewhat" with the court's decision, while 35 percent disagreed. Fifty-four percent of Americans did not agree that the parents should have been allowed by a court to overrule her husband Michael Schiavo's decision, and an even larger 75 percent objected to Congress's involvement in the case (*Time* magazine poll, March 2005).

In the second case, which was not too dissimilar medically from Terri Schiavo's situation, the Nunley family was forced to wrestle with issues in the care of David, an outgoing, intelligent, and athletic young man who in 1989 suffered a severe head injury from a motorcycle accident that left him severely brain damaged. Like Mrs. Schiavo, David was declared to be in a persistent vegetative state, and doctors suggested that it would be an ethically acceptable decision to discontinue his feeding and hydration. Yet, due to the indomitable hope and faith of his mother, Leone, David survived the accident and the medical complications that followed. Today, he is a functioning individual, giving and receiving love, and although he has never returned to the state he was in before the accident, David has a meaningful life.

What is the difference between the case of Terri Schiavo and that of David? Perhaps more than anything else, Leone's boundless maternal love and faith caused her to continue hoping and trying, first simply to keep him alive, and later to provide him therapies to stimulate his damaged brain to recover at least some of its lost function. Terri Schiavo's case, sadly, was very different. According to medical records, Michael stopped providing his wife, Terri, with rehabilitative therapy in 1994, while David McRae continues to receive vigorous therapy to this day.

Leone Nunley correctly observes that the debate about Terri Schiavo's feeding tube should be secondary to the more important issue of the sort of therapy the brain-damaged woman received, and it seems one must conclude that Mrs. Schiavo's therapy was abandoned too early. Leone Nunley is not opposed to the removal of feeding tubes in principle, but she believes that every effort should be made to ascertain the patient's potential and provide whatever therapy is possible. The ethics of withdrawing feeding tubes is indeed controversial. Where does the Christian medical/ethical community stand on this issue? Are artificial feeding and hydration simply provisions of basic care to the thirsty and hungry, and thus ethically necessary according to Matthew 25:34-46? Or are they examples of "heroic measures" or "extraordinary care" that may be withheld or withdrawn if they seem to be providing no real benefit to the patient? Some, such as ethicist Gilbert Meilaender and Pope John Paul II, have insisted that such care be always given, while other Christian bioethicists regard them as optional treatments that ethically may be withdrawn. In fact, the membership of the Christian Medical Association is divided on this issue, according to its executive director, Dr. David Stevens.

Cases like those of Terri Schiavo and David raise difficult issues for our society. Increasingly, medical technology is able to prolong lives far longer than before, but along with this blessing come the costs of human suffering and economic expense. It is essential that we respect the great gift of human life and protect *all* people, since each one is created in God's image and therefore has genuine dignity. Humanity should not be discarded simply because care has become difficult or expensive: Each life is of incalculable value. In particular, we must resist the economic pressure to end lives simply because of the costs imposed by caring for them. Approximately one-fourth of Medicare expenditures go to pay for care in the final year of life. It may become all too tempting to get rid of the weak, the unproductive, and the defective in an age that seems to worship fitness, success, and beauty. In insisting on care for such as these, Christians find themselves with helpful allies in the disability community and organizations such as Not Dead Yet.

While it is important to affirm the dignity of all people and the worth of every life, it is equally important as Christians to recognize that this earthly life is not all that there is. Because of our assurance of eternal life, we need not cling to biological life at all costs. Instead, we need to think carefully about our wishes for the sort of care we would desire should we lose the ability to make or communicate decisions. Each of us needs to discuss these issues in our churches and in our families. Those closest to us, who someday may be asked to make decisions on our behalf, need to know exactly how we feel about being on a ventilator or a feeding tube, or receiving aggressive cardiopulmonary resuscitation (CPR) and other medical interventions. We may wish to create a living will (if it is legally recognized in our state) and to put as many decisions in writing as possible. More important, we should consider designating through Durable Power of Attorney for Health Care someone whom we authorize to make decisions for us when we can no longer make them for ourselves. The document "Five Wishes" has been helpful for stimulating discussion on these matters, and it can be used in most states as a legal document to express a person's wishes for medical care.[1]

Of course, David McRae was injured before end-of-life issues were commonly discussed. Fortunately, he was surrounded by family who recognized his worth and dignity and made the best decisions they could on his behalf. *Fighting for David* is a story of triumph over overwhelming medical complications, sometimes-unsympathetic medical staff, obstinate insurance companies and bureaucrats, doubts, and personal fatigue. Significantly, David's survival and partial recovery could not have happened without the sacrificial love of the people of the Nunleys' church, who provided years of dedicated spiritual support and practical, hands-on care. This book is a wonderful account of God's people stepping up to the task of providing difficult support over a long period of time and is a witness to the reality of Christian community. David's story shows that the decision to sustain a damaged life such as his is far from easy; it is a commitment to a grueling, frustrating series of ordeals and trials. Yet, as this book shows, his mother, Leone, would not have made any other choice.

David B. Fletcher, PhD, teaches philosophy at Wheaton College, Wheaton, Illinois, and bioethics at Trinity International University, Deerfield, Illinois.

ONE

The Sunday the Sun Went Dark

The images on our bedroom TV had me riveted. Throughout the winter of 2004 and early spring of 2005, the networks were playing and replaying footage of Terri Schiavo, the brain-injured Florida woman who had mysteriously collapsed fifteen years before and who now spent her days lying in an institutional bed while lawyers and judges debated the removal of her food and water.

Every time I watched the footage of Terri's mother, Mary Schindler, reaching down to caress her daughter, my heart would break. How many times had I leaned down to embrace my son David the very same way?

Seeing the pictures of Terri lying forlorn and without hope kicked my soul into overdrive. Didn't people understand that if you forsake someone in this condition, of course she would go downhill? I learned that Terri had received no therapy for more than a decade. She spent her days and nights in a darkened room. She had been, to use one observer's chilling term, "warehoused." How could she ever make progress under those conditions—feeding tube or not?

I suddenly knew what I had to do. I had to get in touch with Terri's family. I had to let them know about David. I had to tell them that there was hope.

Like the Schindlers, our lives had been shattered by a phone call. There was no hint of the upheaval to come that sparkling October morning, as the blue-green waters slapped gently onto Kamaole Beach just across the road from our second-floor apartment. The temperature was a balmy seventy-five degrees, headed for a high in the mideighties, even as our families back on the mainland were raking leaves and preparing for the winter of 1989. Here on the island of Maui, I expected just another normal day in paradise.

Actually, I hadn't had time to look out the window at the ocean beauty yet; I was too busy getting myself and the rest of the family ready to leave for church. Dale, my husband, had made coffee early, as he always did. Bill, fifteen, and Steve, our seven-year-old, had each grabbed a bowl of cereal.

I stepped into my short-sleeved dress and did a hurried makeup job on my face. "Are you guys ready yet?" I called from the bedroom as I checked the mirror again.

"Sure, Mom—what about *you*?" Bill hollered back.

"Okay, let's get moving," Dale's baritone voice announced. "It's almost 10:30."

We stepped out onto the landing, and Dale locked the front door. Across the way, we could see slant-walled condos in various stages of completion; my husband was the construction manager for this development of three hundred units, which is why we were living here for a year instead of back in our hometown of Yakima, in central Washington. The sun shone brilliantly on the palm trees that swayed above the barbecue pits.

We turned toward the stairs . . . when, through the open window, we heard the phone ring.

"Don't answer it," somebody said. "We're going to be late."

But being the compulsive mother I am, I just couldn't walk away. "Oh, it's probably David," I said, unlocking the door. My twenty-one-year-old son, now a junior at Washington State University, had called the evening before. We'd had a pleasant conversation, eventually getting around to the subject of how much he'd charged on his credit card (really neat gifts for his girlfriend, you understand). He wondered if I could help him out with some extra cash.

We had talked about how much money he had in mind, and in the end I had made no promises. "Well, just hang in there, Dave—I'm flying back home next Tuesday for Grandpa and Grandma's fiftieth wedding anniversary party. We can talk about it then."

"Okay, Mom," he had replied. "I'll call you again tomorrow though. Bye—I love you!"

"I love you, too, Son."

Now on Sunday morning, I reached for the phone, expecting to hear his cheerful greeting. But it was not David.

An unfamiliar male voice said, "Hello, I'm calling for Leone Nunley. Would that be you?"

"Yes."

With serious professionalism, the man continued, "I'm Dr. T. W. Hill calling from Lewiston, Idaho; I'm a neurosurgeon here at St. Joseph Regional Medical Center. We have a David McRae here—is that your son?"

"Yes! What's wrong?!" I cried.

"Apparently he was in a major motorcycle accident this morning just north of town. He has sustained a life-threatening head injury. We're doing the best we can to stabilize him, but I have to say he's not stable at the present moment. You need to get here as soon as possible. In fact, I really can't guarantee that he will make it until you get here."

"Nooooo! Nooooo!" I wailed as I crumpled to my knees on the hallway floor. "Oh, no . . . my David!" I sobbed.

"I'm very sorry," Dr. Hill replied. "Can you fly here immediately?"

"Yes . . . I . . . what . . . I . . ." My words were slipping into incoherence. *That stupid motorcycle!* I hadn't wanted him to buy it in the first place. But he had given me the typical "Aw, Mom, I'll be careful" speech that thousands of mothers have heard over the years.

I caught my breath enough to ask the doctor a follow-up question: "Does he have any other injuries? Any broken bones?"

"No, apparently not," he explained. "He had dressed pretty warmly for the ride down from Pullman [thirty miles north, where the university is] since it's getting chilly here. Several layers. That protected his limbs, so he has only a couple of abrasions. He was wearing his helmet, which was cracked from the impact of his landing on his head. All the damage is inside the cranium. That's our major problem."

Once again I shuddered with a fresh flow of tears. *My son!* I could hardly catch my breath. The blood began pounding in my ears.

"Well, I'll get there as soon as I can," I pledged, and with that, the conversation ended.

I turned around to see the stricken faces of my husband and the boys staring at me from the kitchen. Dale rushed to my side and helped me stand up. "What happened?" everybody asked at once.

"David had an accident on his motorcycle, and he's in critical condition!" I could barely get the words out. "That was a doctor from Lewiston, Idaho. He doesn't even know if David will last until we get there." I fell onto Dale's shoulder and shook with grief.

They wanted more details, of course, but I had few to offer. I looked at my husband through flooded eyes, pleading with him to take charge, to tell me what to do next.

He thought for a moment, then turned to Bill and said, "Take your little brother across to the beach for a while. Your mother and I need to talk."

With that, the boys disappeared.

"What all did he hurt?" Dale asked, trying to gather facts. His eyes were soft and caring.

"His head!" I cried. "He has a horrible head injury. Oh, what are we going to do? He should have had the Buick up there at college!" I was referring to the family sedan we'd left behind in Yakima.

Dale didn't bother pointing out that a twenty-one-year-old would hardly go to college driving a bulky Buick. Instead, a heavy sigh escaped Dale's lips as his mind laid strategy. "You go start packing," he ordered, "and I'll call the airlines."

At that moment, neither one of us had an accurate sense of the time difference between Hawaii and the mainland. It was already early afternoon in Washington and the panhandle of Idaho, which were three time zones ahead of us in Hawaii. For Dr. Hill even to find us had been an ordeal; all that was known in the beginning, from the wallet in David's back pocket, was that he was from Yakima. A phone call to the Yakima police chaplain proved fortuitous, in that he was a member of West Side Baptist Church where we had also attended. He immediately knew we were in Hawaii for this construction job, and he knew how to reach Bud, the oldest of my boys. From there the contact information flowed back to Lewiston, until Dr. Hill dialed our number.

I packed in a frenzy, not even thinking about how my Hawaii wardrobe would leave me shivering in northern Idaho's fall weather. I didn't notice when the two boys came back from the beach. Within minutes Dale and I were ready to head for the small airport at Lahaina, some eighteen miles away, which in those days still had commuter flights to Honolulu International Airport. A neighbor volunteered to drive us.

"You guys just stay here," Dale instructed Bill and Steve as he picked up my suitcase. "I'll be back in an hour or so after I get Mom on the plane."

We went screeching around the curves of the ocean-side highway at breakneck speeds. To be honest, I can't remember there being much conversation in the car. My mind was a blur of anguish, unanswered questions, and worry. How could this have happened to David? He'd been every parent's dream for a son.

At the airport, we raced inside. Dale went to the desk and got my first ticket, while I hurried to a pay phone and called both our mothers in Portland, Oregon, hysterically passing along the news. Within minutes I kissed Dale good-bye and found my seat on the little four-engine prop that would make the twenty-minute trip to Honolulu.

While we were waiting for the plane to move away from the terminal and head for the runway, a young airline employee ran out to give me a message. Crouching down beside my seat, he said in a low voice, "They just got another update on your son. He's somewhat stabilized now."

"Oh, thank you!" I cried. I had no idea how this message had been passed along to reach me, but I was glad for any glimmer of good news.

He had no sooner walked away, however, when a new panic struck me. *Once I get to Honolulu, I don't have any tickets for the rest of the way! I'll be stranded there!* In a flash, I jumped up, grabbed my purse, and dashed up the aisle. Just before they closed the door, I flew down the steps and back into the terminal.

"Dale! I don't have any tickets!" I shouted. This was before the days of electronic ticketing, and without a piece of paper in my hand, I knew I'd be stuck.

My husband rolled his eyes, then took my shoulders in his big, calloused hands and controlled himself enough to reply, "Leone—I already told you that I got your tickets all lined up on the phone. They'll be waiting for you at the main desk once you get to Honolulu. Get back on that plane!"

Somehow I hadn't heard that instruction. We whirled around—and to our dismay, saw out the window that the propellers were already moving. I had sabotaged the whole schedule.

"Honey—I'm sorry! I should have known you would have it all figured out. What do we do now?"

We scurried back to the ticket counter and explained our predicament. The airline agents, who were aware of our crisis, quickly rebooked me on the next hop to Honolulu, which would leave in another half hour or so. Dale used the intervening minutes to review with me again my itinerary and how to accomplish it. Soon it was time to say good-bye.

"I'll see if they'll let me use that ticket you already bought for next Tuesday, just changing the name," he explained. "If that works, I'll see you by the middle of the week. I'll ask the Nazzises [our neighbors] if they'll look in on Billy and Steve while I'm gone. Be sure and tell David I love him." We hugged each other, and soon I was in the air.

I stared at the itinerary in my hand and realized that my stupidity in running off of the first flight was going to cost me my connection in Honolulu. The big plane to the mainland would already have left by the time I landed.

But when I entered the terminal, the monitor said the flight to Seattle was running an hour late. It hadn't left after all. I breathed a sigh of relief as I headed for the counter to get the ticket that Dale had promised would be there.

And finally I was seated in the Hawaiian Airlines jumbo jet

awaiting takeoff. I slumped down in my seat. I felt the adrenaline start to drain out of me, even though I was far from calm. What were they doing for David by now? I wondered. Was he any better? Would a hospital in a town that size be big enough to handle his crisis? But the doctor on the phone had sounded really competent. How did they fix a brain injury, anyway? I had no idea.

Five and a half hours is an excruciatingly long time to sit on an airplane with nothing to do while your son is close to death. I couldn't sleep; I had no interest in talking to other people or watching the movie; I wasn't even interested in the meal service. I could only stare out at the vast Pacific Ocean as the engines droned on and on . . . thinking, wondering, and remembering.

David was the third of my five sons, in many ways the easiest of them all to raise. Not that he was docile; in fact, he was a bouncy kid—always on the go, a ball of energy, and nearly always happy. He made good grades in school; he had been honored at the end of high school for academic excellence in science. But he had given just as much energy to sports, playing football until he tore a groin muscle and then turning to wrestling. During our earlier stint in Hawaii (again, for job reasons), back when David was a high school sophomore, he was the state runner-up in the 146-pound class. All the Hawaiian and Samoan guys on the team loved him, even if he was a *haole,* their term for a Caucasian.

He made just as many friends back at East Valley High School in Yakima the next year. Kids loved hearing about his practical jokes. One time he hid behind a dumpster until the principal, Gary Erb, came walking by. Suddenly an eerie, unseen voice called out, "GAAAARRRRRRRRYYY!" The principal never did figure out where it was coming from. The rest of us, however, just roared when David told the story.

After the school day ended, he worked at JCPenney, where I was an interior designer. He absolutely loved chasing down shoplifters, running after them all the way to their cars. To him, it was great fun. His pranks at work were legendary. One time he propped up a mannequin behind the door of the package pickup department especially for the benefit of June, a woman in her sixties who worked there. When she came in, the mannequin absolutely scared her to death. She went straight to the manager to complain that "David McRae just about took the life out of me!" Everybody else thought it was hilarious.

One night just after closing time, David picked up the paging microphone at the switchboard desk and launched into an impromptu rap—not thinking about the fact that a few straggling customers might still be in the store. Again, no harm was done, even if he was slightly embarrassed.

He kept working at Penney's all through his two years at Yakima Valley Community College, where he made the dean's list. I thought back to our last night together the previous summer, just before we headed to Hawaii and he left for Washington State as a junior to study physical therapy. I was still racing around the house getting it ready for the renters when he finally got home from work around ten o'clock. "Hey, Mom— what can I do to help you?" he said. I put him to work cleaning toilets.

Halfway up the stairs, he leaned across the railing to say almost in wonderment, "You know what? I'm going to be out on my own starting tomorrow!"

"That's right, David," I answered with a catch in my throat. "You'll be off to college, and we'll be far away in Hawaii. Whatever gets done, you'll be doing it." Both of us let that sink in for a moment.

And now, just three months later . . . he wasn't moving a muscle there in the ICU. No smile crossed his face, no laugh escaped his lips. Could he even sense pain? Was he still breathing? The cloud of unknowns was driving me crazy. Was he able to pray? Would he have any sense of the Lord being there beside him, though I was not?

David's love for God was up-front and obvious to anyone who knew him at all. But not in a boisterous way. When he said things like, "You know what—I'm sure of where I'm going when I die," people actually believed him. They would sometimes ask him how he knew, and he would answer all about heaven and the way to get there, with utmost sincerity. He could talk about his faith naturally and openly.

Even those who disagreed with his beliefs or moral positions found him likable. The high school teacher who nominated him for the science award certainly didn't see eye to eye with him on some issues, but David's faith was not obnoxious or judgmental.

He took life and relationships in an easy stride, flexing with the punches. Perhaps he learned some of that in the early years of having to cope with his father's alcoholic outbursts. Life when he was young was anything but smooth. Leo McRae had left deep marks on the spirit—and sometimes the body—of David as well as his brothers and me. I had grown up in the home of an alcoholic steelworker myself—and had quit college after one year to marry someone with the same behavior problems as my own father. At the age of twenty-two, as a young wife and mother, I watched Billy Graham on TV one night and realized I needed Christ's help. As the years went by and more children were born, I attended church and took my boys with me—much to their father's disgust. We didn't bend to his protests; we needed the spiritual stamina that God provided for what we were facing.

Finally, after nearly sixteen years of broken promises and broken bones, I announced to the boys that we were making a new start. When the divorce went through, David had just turned nine, Bud was fourteen, Rob was ten and a half, and Bill was just three. I would support them through my job at Penney's.

A couple of years later, a contractor whose homes I was decorating started showing more than just a business interest in me. Dale was six years older, a wonderful man with a marsh-mallow heart underneath his crusty, hard-hat persona. He and I were married on August 25, 1979. He had four grown sons of his own. Eventually we had Steve when I was forty years old, making nine boys altogether—"our own baseball team," as Dale liked to say . . . except that now, one of our players had been carried off the field on a stretcher.

In my distraught condition, the only verse of Scripture I could muster up in my head on that long flight was the familiar John 3:16: "For God so loved the world that he gave his one and only Son. . . ." God knew what it was like to surrender a son to pain and death. I hoped against hope that I wouldn't have to do the same. I reminded myself that the first part of the verse assured me that God loved the world greatly. That world included me. *Oh, Lord, please protect us from further tragedy,* I prayed silently. *Please spare David's life. Please keep him alive until I get there.*

The sky grew dark outside the aircraft window as we neared Sea-Tac Airport at last. The pilot came walking back to where I sat. "Are you Leone Nunley?" he asked.

"Yes."

"Well, I just wanted you to know that as soon as we come to a stop at the gate, you'll be escorted right out to the ramp ahead of everyone else. We've got the Lewiston flight holding for you, to make sure you get your connection. Otherwise you'd be spending the night in Seattle, because there are no later flights."

"Oh, thank you so much," I replied.

I was whisked away to another gate in a matter of minutes to board the much smaller plane to Lewiston. I stepped through the door to see row upon row of somber faces. They had been waiting at least half an hour for me. But there was no mumbling or irritation. Only a respectful quietness prevailed. They had obviously been told that I was a woman in crisis, heading into a tragedy. Nobody griped about the delay, even though it was late in the evening.

We bounced our way up and across the Cascade Range and then through the inky sky toward the Lewiston–Nez Perce County Airport. *Soon I will know the truth,* I said to myself. *I wonder what it will be?*

I stepped into the small terminal and quickly spotted my oldest son, Bud, twenty-six, and his wife, Lori. They had driven the four hours from Yakima. We fell into one another's arms for a long hug.

The first words out of my mouth were, "Is he still . . . ?" I couldn't finish the question for fear of hastening a negative answer.

"Yes, Mom, he's still alive," Bud reassured me. "Let's get your luggage and go straight to the hospital."

On the quick ride north through the dark streets toward the center of town, my methodical son began preparing me for what I was about to face. "Now, Mom, you need to know that when we go in there, David will be on a ventilator. There's a big tube in his mouth that's doing the breathing for him. They've got him on some very powerful drugs to keep him entirely still. I mean, he was already unconscious when the medics brought him in from the accident, but now they've got him that way on purpose. They don't want any stimulation to increase the swelling in his brain.

"He's wired up to all kinds of other machines. And just brace yourself—he's not moving at all. You won't get any response from him for now. He's absolutely *out*."

It was near midnight when we walked into the quiet hospital. The front desk was unattended at that hour; the reception chairs were empty. We approached the intensive care unit. Doctors had gone home, leaving the overnight nursing crew in charge.

A nurse stood up from her station. "Mrs. Nunley?" she asked.

"Yes."

"I'll take you to see your son. He's in a very deep coma, you know. For now, we just have to wait and see."

She gently guided me into the ICU. And there, at last, I saw my son, an ashen figure lying corpselike on the bed with his eyes closed, while technology blinked and hissed on all sides. My hands flew to cover my mouth as I gasped, my eyes filling with tears. I thought I might collapse from the gruesome sight before me.

But I willed myself to stay on my feet and edged toward his side. With one hand I gripped the bed rail, while with the other I reached out to touch his arm.

"David, it's Mom," I whispered, not knowing if he could even hear me. "I'm here. I got here as fast as I could."

He showed no sign, no twitch or flicker of hearing my words or recognizing my voice. All remained still, frozen in place.

"Oh, David, I'm so sorry!" I continued. "I love you so much." I kept stroking his hand, wanting desperately for him to know he wasn't alone. Could he tell?

"Bud and Lori are here too. We're all pulling for you, David. We're praying for you. . . ." I stared into his face, the face that had always been so animated and energetic, laughing and joking and communicating. Now it was a stone.

I turned to the nurse. "What do all these dials mean? What are they telling you?"

She motioned toward the ventilator and explained that its gauge showed how much oxygen was being pumped into David. She reviewed what medicines were going in through the IVs. She pointed to the vital-signs monitor with green lines moving across a screen, which displayed his heart rate and blood pressure readings.

"And this line," she continued, "monitors the pressure

inside the cranium. The surgeon put a device into his skull to measure how much swelling we're facing. As far as we can tell, there isn't a lot of internal bleeding, but the swelling is quite severe. As you can see, his pressure reading is around 17 or 18. That's not good. Normal would be down around 5 or 6.

"Actually, we should step back outside to keep talking," she then said. "The less stimulation for David, the better at this stage."

I didn't want to leave his side. But reluctantly, I followed her out of the room. We retreated to the waiting area, where I asked more questions. Some of them she could answer, but others were met only with "I'm sorry, but I'm not the person to give an opinion on that. Ask Dr. Hill when you talk with him tomorrow."

"When can I go back in to be with him again?" I asked.

"We've been directed to limit the visits to just two minutes every two hours for now," she replied. My face dropped in dismay. "I'm really sorry," she said with empathy. With that, she returned to her station.

Bud, Lori, and I remained in the waiting room. We were all more or less in a state of shock. Hardly anyone spoke. We huddled in our own little shells, deep in thought and prayer. This was by far the worst thing that had ever happened in my nearly forty-eight years. *What if he never wakes up?* I worried. *What if he turns out to be a vegetable? Will he ever get back to normal?* My emotions were swelling like a turbulent ocean, and I didn't know how to calm them.

"What was he doing down here in Lewiston on his motorcycle on a Sunday morning anyway?" I suddenly blurted out.

Bud knew at least some of the answer to that one. "They

say he was on his way to a new job at PayLess Drug Store. He'd done the training up in the Pullman store near the university, and this was going to be his first day of actual work. He was riding the motorcycle because his Triumph Spitfire wasn't running—*again*." We all knew the trials he had gone through trying to keep that little sports car functional; something always seemed to be wrong with it.

After a while, the nurse came over to say, "You know, this hospital has a hospice across the street with rooms for out-of-town family members to use. We've reserved rooms for you folks if you want to go get some rest." I knew I looked a wreck after this marathon day, and she no doubt thought I could benefit from some sleep.

"No, we'll just stay here," I announced. "When can we go back in to see David?"

She checked her watch. "At 2 a.m.," she replied. "Again, I'm sorry, but it's really for the best."

We spent the rest of the night in those brown-striped armchairs, immobilized by our trauma. I had sat in rooms like this plenty of times during David's growing-up years, when he'd needed stitches for a scrape or treatment for some other injury; he had in fact been our accident-prone child. But tonight's ordeal was of a whole different magnitude. I was teetering on the edge of losing my son altogether, and I thought my heart would break. What an incredible gift he had been up to this point. If he slipped away from us in the next hour, the next day, the next week, I did not think I could go on living. The blackness of the Idaho night was duplicated in the despair of my soul.

TWO

From Bad to Worse

When the sun came up the next morning, the hospital corridors quickly resumed their busy pace. The day shift of nurses arrived to review their caseloads, while carts of breakfast trays emerged from elevators and doctors began making their early rounds.

Soon a medium-height man with light hair and wearing a lab coat came walking toward me. He was perhaps in his forties and seemed very confident. "Hello, I'm Dr. Hill," he said. "It's good to see that you made it all the way from Hawaii. What time did you arrive?"

"About midnight," I answered, reaching out to shake his hand. "Thank you for calling; I know it was hard to find us."

"Yes, I'm glad I got through to you."

He had already checked on David that morning

and quickly began giving me an update. "Your son remained stable through the night, even though his condition is very grave," he said. "I've seen the results of the CT scan over in radiology, and it shows what I expected: a coup-contrecoup injury. The brain, as you know, is a soft organ that resides inside the hard shell of the skull. When a sudden impact occurs, the brain at first slams toward the skull wall, causing some damage—but then it rebounds the opposite direction and hits the other side of the skull, injuring that part as well." Dr. Hill motioned with his head to illustrate.

"It appears that David hit the pavement on the right side of his head—the coup impact—but the more serious damage is in the *left* temporal lobe—in other words, the contrecoup part of things.

"Of course, there is diffuse edema—swelling—all throughout the brain, which is what is causing the increased pressure. That's our real concern. We're doing everything we can to bring that under control. And keeping him sedated is all part of the strategy.

"Do you have any questions I might answer?"

I hardly knew what to say. The whole thought of brain injury had always made me shudder. It had to be the absolute worst thing that could happen to a person's body. The only query I could come up with was, "Do you think he'll be all right eventually?"

Dr. Hill paused, as if to choose his words with care. "It's much too soon to say," he finally replied. "There's a lot we can't know for now. When he arrived here yesterday around eleven o'clock, he evidenced what we call 'decerebrate posturing'—rigid arms and legs, toes pointed downward, and head

thrown back. As you see now, at least that has ceased. We just
have to keep watching and waiting for more developments."

And with that, he stood up to move on to the rest of his
busy schedule. It was hard for me not to have a clear plan of
action to follow. I wanted somebody to say, "We'll do this, and
this, and then this, and at the end of such and such a time, your
son will be fixed." But it wouldn't be that simple.

I went looking for a phone so I could call Dale and tell him
what little I knew. It was reassuring to hear his voice. He told
me he had succeeded in getting onto the Tuesday flights,
which meant he would see me sometime Wednesday. He said
the church had already volunteered to bring meals for the boys
while he was gone, since they would have to stay there for
school. "Don't worry, honey," he concluded. "They'll be okay,
and I'll be with you in just two days."

I then returned to the ICU nurses' station, pleading for as
much time with David as they would allow. He looked the
same as when I had arrived the night before—comatose,
unmoving, unaware. At every visit, I would stare at him, stroke
his hand, stroke his feet, and tell him I loved him so very much.
I had no idea whether he could hear me or not. But I would
talk to him anyway. And then, all too soon, the nurse would
signal that I must leave again.

My energy was drooping after a night of almost no sleep,
but I couldn't go. In between my bedside vigils, I was buoyed
by the phone calls from Yakima that started to pour in. Friends
from the church, neighbors, fellow employees from Penney's,
business contacts of Dale's—they all wanted to find out the latest news and to tell me they were thinking of us. What a
strength those calls were to me. They let me know we were

not alone. The hospital staff eventually joked that maybe they needed to put in a private line just for us.

What Actually Happened?

Late that day, a call came from a stranger. "You don't know me," the young-sounding woman started out, "but my name is Linda Sharp. I was at the accident scene just after it happened, and I haven't been able to think about another thing since. I had to call to find out how your son is doing."

"Well, he's in a coma, and he's not doing very well," I replied. "The main damage is to his head. There are no other injuries or broken bones that we know of."

But what I really wanted was to hear her story. "Tell me what you saw," I added. This would be my first contact with an eyewitness.

She began to talk about how she and her three young children had spent Saturday night with a friend in Lewiston, and they were headed back north that Sunday morning to go to church. "When we came up to the top of the Lewiston Grade—suddenly, there was your son lying right on the double yellow line! His smashed-up motorcycle was off to one side, and the other car was parked in the grass, with the driver standing alongside holding a baby girl."

(Lewiston, I should explain, sits in a valley at the junction of the Clearwater and Snake Rivers, along with its twin city, Clarkston, Washington, just across the state line. This was a stopover for the famous Lewis and Clark Expedition of 1804 to 1806, which is how the two towns got their names. Opposite the towns, a steep ridge rises some two thousand feet above the valley floor. U.S. 95 winds to the top of this ridge and then divides right at the state line. U.S. 95 keeps going northeast toward Moscow, Idaho, while U.S. 195 splits off northwest toward Pullman and Spokane, Washington. This junction was where tragedy struck.)

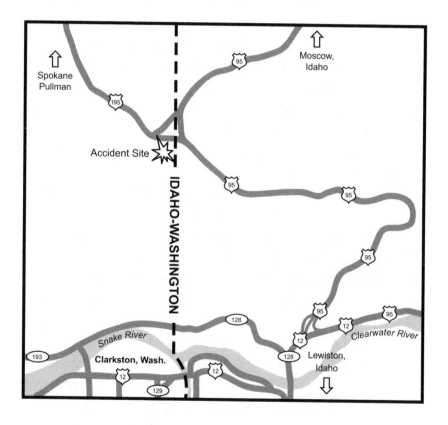

Linda Sharp had not actually seen the impact, although I learned the facts a bit later from the state patrol. The driver of a '77 Oldsmobile Cutlass was coming down from Pullman, with David riding somewhat behind him. The man, instead of proceeding on to Lewiston, wanted to bear left to the northeast toward Moscow, his home. But he missed his turn—and then suddenly slowed down in the roadway to figure out how to remedy his problem. David swerved to miss him but couldn't react fast enough to avoid clipping the back of the car, which catapulted him through the air a sickening distance of thirty-nine feet. He slammed headfirst into the pavement and skidded another twenty feet before stopping.

"This was out in the middle of nowhere," Linda continued. "Only one man had stopped to help before me. He was bent down, just rolling David over, when I pulled up. I could see your son in a tan flannel jacket with thick quilted lining, and he had on insulated riding pants. The only blood was just a little coming from one nostril. But the face guard was absolutely shredded, from the right jaw area to the middle.

"It was horrible. I rolled down my window and yelled to the man, 'Has anybody called an ambulance?' He said no and asked if I would do that."

Linda then went flying up the road in search of a phone. At the first house, about a quarter mile north, she found a group of young guys who apparently had been partying all Saturday night; they obviously weren't going to be of much help. She drove on another half mile to a farmhouse and started banging on the front door. Just then a man came out of the barn. He brought her inside to call the Washington State Patrol. He also volunteered to go back to the accident scene with her, bringing some blankets, because the temperature was only in the high thirties.

"When we got back, the first man removed David's helmet, which was a mess," Linda continued. "David didn't flinch at anything; he didn't open his eyes. There was no expression at all. His face was absolutely pale.

"I thought it was interesting that the other driver would not come near David. He just stayed over by his car, holding his baby—a little girl about ten months old. He made no comment, no response—maybe he was in shock. I gave him one of my son's bottles and also some diapers I had along.

"We moved David just enough to get his wallet out of his back pocket. There I saw his driver's license, with that good-looking picture. I realized he must be a college student from Yakima.

"Finally, another man stopped—an older gentleman. He said he was a doctor; he looked as if he might be retired. He bent down over David, and then he said something that just sent chills down my spine: 'He's not going to make it if he doesn't get to a good neurosurgeon within an hour. And he probably won't make it anyway.'"

Linda started to choke up as she told what happened next. "I burst into tears. I said to myself, *Oh no—he can't die without his mother! Nobody this young should die without their mom!* I took off his right glove and held his hand, rubbing it as I quietly prayed and prayed and prayed for him to keep living somehow.

"See, I'm probably still emotional from the birth of my own son just three months ago. The mother-son bond is just so fresh in my mind. I couldn't stand the thought of him dying without you being at his side."

By now I was crying too. "Thank you, thank you, thank you!" I responded. "That just means the world to me, that you stopped and comforted him. I don't know how to thank you enough."

"Well, I just had to do it," Linda said. "The ambulance finally came and took him away. I drove on to church with my kids, but when we went inside, I couldn't concentrate. I took my kids and went home again. I just sat the rest of the day in my rocking chair holding my infant son."

Then suddenly her voice strengthened. "Leone, I just want to say one more thing to you." She paused. Then, "I saw the situation with my own eyes, and *that accident could not have been David's fault.*"

I heard what she said, but to be honest, I didn't pay a lot of attention in that moment. I was too consumed with the current crisis. I did remember to pass the comment along to Dale when he arrived, however.

Uninsured?

Sometime Monday I stopped by St. Joseph's business office to sign insurance paperwork on behalf of David. I showed them his insurance membership card as part of our family policy provided by Dale's employer in Hawaii.

The rest of Monday was spent at David's bedside as much as possible. Every time I would walk into his space in the ICU, my first glance would not be toward him but toward the brain pressure monitor. The numbers weren't lessening; unfortunately, they seemed to be creeping ever higher. I worried about that, and I could tell that the nurses were concerned too.

By that evening, I finally let Bud and Lori coax me across the street to the hospice quarters for some sleep. It wasn't easy;

my heart wanted to be as close to David around the clock as I could be. But I knew that without rest, I couldn't keep functioning at this intensity. The hospice room was pleasantly furnished, and Bud and Lori were right next door.

Early Tuesday morning I was back at the hospital again. David had made it through another night. Otherwise, there was nothing to rejoice over. His eyes were still closed, his color was still dreadful, and he was completely unresponsive, no matter how many times I asked him to blink or to squeeze my hand. Nothing at all.

Sometime that day, the business office asked me to stop by again. When I sat down with the account manager there, she said, "Um, it looks like we have a problem. We called your insurance company, and they said David is not covered under this policy."

"What?! He most certainly is! I even showed you his card!"

"Yes, I know. It's strange—because they said their coverage stops at a dependent's nineteenth birthday, unless they keep living under your roof and you pay all their bills. David's twenty-one now."

"But he's a full-time college student! And why did they give him his card?" I demanded, my blood pressure rising. "It even says his birth date right here on the card: 02-68. It's now October 1989. They obviously knew how old he was when they printed it last spring. This is crazy!"

To me, this was absolutely the end of the world. My son was lying comatose with a life-threatening brain injury, and this nationally known insurance company was refusing to pay the bills?

"Don't panic, Mrs. Nunley," the woman kindly said. "We'll

keep working for clarification on this. If in fact it turns out that David is uninsured, then the alternative will be for him to go on Medicaid. We'll help set you up to see Social Security and apply for that if need be."

I had to just let the mystery go until Dale arrived the next day. Otherwise I would have gone stark-raving mad. He would know what to do. And at least the hospital didn't seem upset. They weren't about to throw us out the door.

Dale was in fact airborne as we spoke, heading for Seattle and then on to Yakima. He arrived late that evening, intending to pick up our waiting Buick and drive on to Lewiston so we'd have more transportation options. While in town he immediately got in touch with the manager he had left in charge of his Yakima company, Four Suns Construction, while we were away for the year in Hawaii. They began reviewing the state of the business.

The more Dale heard, the more alarmed he became. His manager had not kept him informed on a number of projects. The company had borrowed loads of money to build houses on speculation that Dale had never heard about, let alone approved. Late into the night, Dale kept analyzing the books and realizing his once-healthy business was now on the edge of bankruptcy. What could he do to save it?

All this consumed the next day and was still heavy on his mind as he drove across eastern Washington that Thursday to meet me. *When it rains, it pours,* he thought to himself. David was in the fight of his life to keep from dying, and meanwhile, the family business was about to go belly-up. At least we still had $25,000 in a California bank that could be pulled to appease the creditors. But would it be enough?

The minute he saw me in Lewiston, I hit him with the newest blow: "They say David's not insured on our policy! What in the world is the matter with that company?"

Dale immediately grasped the gravity of the situation. Searching his memory, he replied, "I did get a couple of phone calls awhile back saying there was a problem with David because he was past nineteen, and Kamaole Joint Ventures [the Hawaii employer] didn't have a student plan as part of their package. I said, 'Then how come you enrolled him in the first place? I've got the paperwork right here—the welcome packet, the list of people in our family including him, the wallet card, the whole nine yards.' They mumbled something about 'a computer oversight'—one of those deals, you know. I told them in no uncertain terms that it was too late for them to be backing out now, and they'd better change their records. They said they'd look into it—and that's the last I ever heard!"

"Well, they're singing a different tune to the hospital—now that we need coverage," I answered. "You can talk to them directly, now that you're here."

Before any of that, however, Dale wanted to see David. We entered the ICU together. His reaction was the same as mine had been: stunned silence and tear-filled eyes. He loved this stepson as dearly as any of his own sons. He felt terrible that it had taken him four days to arrive at my side.

In time, Dale stopped at the business office to delve further into the insurance problem. The company was still stonewalling. We faxed in a formal protest. With the hospital's guidance, we went together to the local Social Security Administration office to apply for Medicaid, just in case we lost the insurance battle in the end. They were very helpful, and the financial crisis was abated for the time being.

We had no idea how high the medical bills had already mounted; we were afraid to ask. We focused our attention instead on what was happening—or not happening—at David's bed. We watched and hoped and prayed and searched in vain for any hint of improvement.

Friday Night Crisis

Every day we called the boys back in Hawaii to give updates, of course. We spared them the worst details, however, not wanting to traumatize them. They had enough to cope with, staying in the apartment by themselves. They would ask, "How's David today?" and we'd give a summary report. Then they'd go on to tell about their day at school, what Mrs. Nazzise or someone else from church had brought over to eat, and when the next big game was.

We were also in touch with my second-oldest son, Rob, who was stationed in South Carolina with the navy. Thank goodness he was not out at sea just then. His commanding officer had quickly arranged for emergency leave, so Rob showed up from the east on Wednesday, the same day Dale arrived from the west. Once again, I felt strengthened by the presence of another loved one.

Rob and David had always been extremely close, since they were only eighteen months apart. Rob admitted to me years later that when he saw his younger brother that day, with tubes running everywhere, his first thought was, *This is terminal. There's no way. But—I need to be positive for Mom.* He just put his arm around me and let me know he was there to support us all.

When I explained to Rob what the various monitors were tracking and how the most critical danger we faced was the rising brain pressure, he nodded soberly. We prayed together then, and afterward, that God would somehow relieve this menace.

Thursday passed, and we moved into Friday with still no indication of hope. Neither Dale's voice nor Rob's voice triggered any response from David. It had now been a full five days since the devastating accident.

Around the dinner hour that Friday evening, Dr. Hill asked to talk with us. His face was taut as he said, "The intracranial pressure is now moving into the 40s. I have to tell you, this young man is going to die unless we release that pressure surgically. The cortex—the outer layer of the brain that is so strategic in receiving input from the eyes, ears, and other senses, then deciding what to do with it—is being pushed so hard against the inside of the skull that it's going to shut down altogether if we don't do something. The option is to go in and remove some of the damaged tissue as well as the buildup of fluid, thereby allowing for more space.

"But—the risks of this kind of operation are major. He might not survive the procedure. He might survive but never wake up. He might be left in what we call a 'persistent vegetative state.' On the other hand, we might be more successful than we think. It's impossible to know at this stage."

I shook my head in bewilderment. They were talking about taking out *part of David's brain*! I could hardly fathom something so ghastly. But if we said no . . . we might lose him altogether.

I looked up at Dr. Hill and asked the familiar question that doctors hear frequently: "Well . . . if this were your son, what would you do?"

He quietly responded, "I would go for the surgery."

I answered, "Then I say we go for the surgery. But could we have just a little time as a family to pray about this?"

"Time is definitely of the essence," Dr. Hill said. "Five minutes?"

I nodded, and with that, he walked away.

We looked at each other with blank faces. Nobody wanted to speak first. Were we going to lose David either way? So many unknowns.

"To me, this represents our only hope," I volunteered.

Dale spoke next. "I agree."

Bud looked up and said, in his careful way, "I'm with you, Mom."

Lori, being the new in-law in the family, kept quiet.

Rob said, "I believe in a mother's instincts. If you feel this is what we need to do, Mom, let's do it."

We then got down on our knees, the five of us in a circle there in the waiting room, and prayed together. We pleaded with God to somehow use this surgery to spare David's life.

Meanwhile, the surgical team was springing into action. There was a flurry of preparation; it was obvious they had no time to waste. Soon David's bed was being wheeled out of the ICU and toward the elevator that would take him to the surgical floor.

"You can come along," an orderly said to me as he waited for the doors to open. Someone handed me a consent form, and I scribbled my signature.

Dale and I squeezed into the elevator alongside our son as the orderly pressed the button. We began to move. I looked down once again at David's vacant face and his closed eyes. I lifted my hands to sweep them back and forth a foot or so above his body as I softly prayed through my tears, "Oh, Lord, please help him get through this surgery. He's in such a critical state. Please help Dr. Hill. Please cause this to help David somehow. Please, Lord . . . please."

Then the doors opened into the surgical wing, and he was gone.

THREE

Ice Blankets and Feeding Tubes

Sitting in a waiting room while a loved one is going through major surgery is one of life's great tribulations, as anyone who has done it knows. Your mind has nothing productive to do. You stare into space, imagining a hundred outcomes. What did the surgeon say in his explanation? Inevitably you forget crucial parts of his speech, unless he used such obtuse medical language that you didn't understand him in the first place.

You wonder if walking around would be helpful. You stand up and begin to pace the room, only to return to your seat after a few minutes.

On the end tables are outdated magazines. You glance their way, but somehow it seems silly, even disrespectful, to distract yourself with their trivia. A drama far more weighty is taking place in the other room at

this moment. You wish you could know how it is unfolding—
but then again, too much detail would traumatize you.

You catch the smell of stale coffee from the refreshment
counter. It turns your stomach. You have no appetite. How
long has it been already? Only forty minutes? You still have
more than an hour to endure. Your agitation grows. And then
you feel guilty for being impatient, when others are working
so hard on behalf of your loved one's life. You sink back into
your private stupor.

Dale and the kids were as subdued as I was that Friday
night, waiting for the surgery to finish and for the news to be
announced. It was past ten o'clock when Dr. Hill emerged, still
clad in his green operating gown and cap, a mask hanging
loosely from his neck. We held our breath to hear what he
would say.

"Everything went well," he started out. "We removed some
of the left temporal lobe and drained off some fluid, so that his
ICP [intracranial pressure] reading is way down now, out of the
danger zone."

"So this is good news?" I said.

He wouldn't commit himself. "Well, again, we just have to
wait and see."

Dr. Hill then explained that he would be leaving for a long-
scheduled vacation the next day, but he assured us that David
would be well taken care of by his colleague Dr. Christopher
Moreno and the hospital staff. I worried a bit about his
absence, but there was nothing I could do. This man had
already given us so much.

"Thank you for everything," I replied. "We'll see you when
you get back."

It was a good thing I couldn't immediately read what Dr. Hill had dictated into his recorder that night before he left the hospital. Only much later did I get a copy of his operative report, with its clinical description of opening up David's skull: "The brain began to pooch out through the dural opening [due to the pressure]. . . . I carried out a subtotal temporal lobectomy removing the anterior five to five and a half centimeters [two-plus inches] of temporal lobe. . . . The temporal lobe had necrotic [dead] tissue and small intracerebral hematoma [blood pockets]. . . ." Down at the bottom of the page came the conclusion that needed no interpretation: "Prognosis is guarded. Patient was returned to the ICU."

This specific area of the brain, I was told, is the speech center. To lose a chunk of the left temporal lobe would certainly mean a blow to David's ability to talk someday. Of course, nobody was guaranteeing at this point that he would ever even regain consciousness, let alone say a word.

We solemnly left the hospital that night for our rooms across the street and tried to sleep. The next day our vigil continued. David's head was now wrapped in a huge white bandage resembling a turban, but he still showed no response to his surroundings.

In fact, by early Sunday morning, the brain pressure monitor was starting to creep upward again. We were all disheartened. The drastic surgery had not solved the problem after all. Dr. Moreno ordered new medications to try to subdue the buildup, while we headed to a local Baptist church for whatever encouragement we could glean.

During the prayer time of that service, I found myself saying to God, *I don't know what else we can do, Lord. We got through the surgery—but there are still problems galore. You know how much I love David. And you love him too. I just need to turn him over to you. You're the only one who can rescue my son from all this.*

In praying this, I did not mean to imply that I would be going "off duty" at this point or in any way abandoning my son. I was simply recognizing that I could not manage this situation alone. Neither I nor the medical experts were equal to the challenge. If David was to survive, God would have to throw his divine power into the equation.

The pastor of this church, Bob Severs, proved to be an amazing friend and comfort to our family as the days went on. More than once he showed up at the hospital with a calming word. I will always appreciate his ministry to us in such a critical hour.

Our pastor from Yakima, Wayne Pickens, was likewise a tremendous support, along with his wife, Bonnie. He called me repeatedly for status reports and to see how I was doing. On a day that seemed especially grim, I confessed that I wasn't hopeful at all. It didn't look to me as if David was going to make it. "You know, Pastor Wayne," I said, "if we lose him, I guess heaven's not such a bad address." He heartily agreed with me, and we began to pray together over the phone. We both knew that if David left us, he would indeed be whole again in a flash.

A Second Trauma

By Monday, October 23, we were deep into a new complication: David wasn't getting enough oxygen into his bloodstream. Ventilator pressure was cranked up. The mix of oxygen likewise was raised, eventually to 100 percent, although the body cannot handle that for very long.

At one point, the staff guessed there might be an embolism—

a clot—in the lungs. If so, blood thinner could not be used to help break up the clot because it would wreak havoc in the area of the brain surgery and David would no doubt die.

But then the mystery was solved by a bronchoscopy. Dr. Gary Thorne put a scope down David's throat and discovered that a suction tube had slipped out of place, allowing the left lung to fill with fluid. In addition, the strong pressure from the ventilator had actually blown a hole in the lung, which meant air was leaking into his chest cavity. We could see the effect: His upper chest and neck were beginning to swell. He looked as if he had a layer of sponge rubber just under his skin. The nurses referred to this as "football neck," as some of the burly NFL linemen seem to have.

Doctors ordered that tubes be inserted between his ribs on each side to help pull out the air as well as some of the infection that was building. As you can imagine, this just added insult to the original injury to his head. We seemed to keep slipping in all the wrong directions.

That second week felt like a never-ending crisis as the battle raged to stabilize David. It was capped on Saturday when the phone rang in our hospice room: "Your son has gone into high stress," a nurse said in an agitated voice. "You need to get over here right away!" Dale and I dashed for the street and up to the front entrance of the hospital. The chaplain as well as Bob Severs, the local pastor, met us at the door, and together we raced upstairs to find our son in the throes of a grand mal seizure.

Suddenly, after nearly two weeks of lying still, David's arms were flailing wildly, pulling at tubes and monitor wires, jerking them away from his body. His legs were kicking, and even though his eyes were still closed, his face grimaced. Dale and I watched in horror.

A nurse gave him an injection of Dilantin, an antiepileptic sedative. Soon he calmed down. I couldn't help wondering if this was the start of a whole new phase for us—the brain triggering violent behavior at unpredictable moments.

Somehow we got through the second weekend, and no more seizures occurred. Monday, October 30, turned out to be a milestone day: David opened his eyes at last! Of course we had been hoping and dreaming of this moment. Next thing he'd smile and say, "Hi, Mom!"—right?

But any joy we might have felt was immediately crushed when I took my first look. His eyes were beet red, and I could tell he didn't know a single thing that was going on. He didn't recognize me; he didn't know where he was; he had not a clue about his circumstances. My heart sank.

While his eyes had been shut for two weeks, we had soothed ourselves with the hope that the real David was inside there all right, just out of our view. Soon he'd connect with us again, we assumed. Now that fantasy was dashed. There was nothing, nothing at all.

"His eyes are terrible!" I cried to Dr. Moreno.

"Well, at least they're open," he replied. "That's more than when he first came in here, don't you think?" I drew little comfort from that. Tomorrow would be Halloween, and my son's visage needed no dressing up for the occasion; he was already ghastly enough.

One of the brain's functions, I learned, is to regulate body temperature. David's was soaring to 103 and 104 degrees, and the ICU staff placed him on an ice blanket to try to bring it down. He lay there shivering, with no clothing but a towel across his midsection. Still the fever raged. If it went much higher, it would further damage his already injured brain.

On Wednesday, a technician arrived to do an electroencephalogram (EEG). The doctors hoped to gain insight into what was really going on inside David's brain and whether they should expect more seizures. The result of this brain scan was grim. In the words of Dr. Stockard's written report:

> The EEG is markedly and diffusely abnormal due to the severe attenuation [lessening] of electrocerebral activity and the absence of any normal background rhythms. The absence of spontaneous or reactive variability and continued very low-voltage generalized arrhythmic delta activity is of grave prognostic significance with respect to the chances of significant recovery of higher cerebral function in this case.

To put all that in layman's terms: His head is really messed up, very little is going on in there—and don't expect things to change.

Time to Give In?

More than two weeks had now passed since the accident. Dale and I will never forget Dr. Hill coming to talk with us in the ICU waiting area. He perched himself on the edge of a desk and said, "You know, we've done our best here with your son. This latest brain test is extremely negative. It shows that he's still in pretty much a vegetative state. His cortex is essentially gone—and that's your basis for higher thinking. It's your executive center, the part that drives you to get things done. If the body is saying, 'I need some water,' it's the cortex that says, 'All right, get up and get moving to find a drink of water.' Without that part, you don't really function."

He stopped for a breath, and I wondered where all this was heading.

"When David was first brought in, there was no way we could have known all this, of course," Dr. Hill continued. "We just concentrated on saving his life. We said, as I told you at the time, that we'd have to wait and see what we have later. Now we know a lot more.

"From what the tests are showing, and from what we can reasonably predict about the future quality of life . . ." Here he paused just a second, then continued, "I would have no problem taking David off the respirator and all life support."

I sucked in a breath. This man, who had worked so hard to repair David's massive injuries, had reached the conclusion that the battle was pointless.

"But—I don't think the family is ready for that," he added, almost as an afterthought. He sincerely didn't want to offend us or push us in any direction from the outside.

Tension hung in the air, until I said, "No, Dr. Hill, I'm not ready to pull the plug at all, if that's what you mean." I didn't have any medical grounds for my statement. I was just being a mom in that moment—a mom whose son needed her to hold on and keep on holding on.

"I understand," he quietly replied. He had given us a carefully worded withdrawal option if we wanted to take it, and I had said no thank you.

"You know," Dale piped up, somewhat relieving the tension

in the air by changing the subject, "I just know deep down that the accident wasn't David's fault."

I turned to look at my husband. "Well, who cares whose fault it was?" I shot back. "What difference does that make?"

"I don't know—I guess it's just all part of the picture," Dale replied. He was thinking strategically in that moment, while I was completely zoned in on the need for ongoing medical care. In the future, the fact that David had a justifiable claim to an insurance settlement from the other driver would prove essential in paying for some of that care. Dale was starting to piece this together in his mind. But the follow-through would have to wait for another day.

Locked Out

That same week, in fact, Dale had to leave and head back to Hawaii. He had been away from the boys and his job too long already. I remember his taking me to a Safeway store to stock up on some snacks for the room before he departed. Rob had long since been required to report back to his navy duties and, in fact, was now in a nuclear submarine in the Atlantic, unable to be contacted at all. Bud and Lori had returned to Yakima, where they were just starting a ministry outreach sponsored by West Side Baptist that served a tough part of town called "the Hole." I was left alone.

I could not bear the thought of being away from David. Every time I would leave the hospital to go across the street to the hospice room, I'd be hit with separation anxiety—I just had to get back there again. What if something happened to David while I was away? I was the only one he had now, and I dared not be delinquent in my attention to him.

One evening around eight o'clock, I was standing by his bed, holding his hand. A nurse was attending to him on the other side. She was quiet this evening; in fact, most of the nursing staff had seemed to stop talking recently. They were polite and professional, but a bit reserved, I felt.

My mind, for some reason, went back to the October 20 brain surgery. "Say, do you know," I asked the nurse, "just how much brain they took out of David?"

I shouldn't have asked such a question in front of my son, because brain-injured patients can often hear more than they let on. But I didn't think about that just then.

The nurse didn't know. She called to her coworker on the other side of the room: "Marianne, did you hear how much brain they took out of David McRae?"

The second nurse had no idea I was within earshot. She bluntly (and incorrectly) answered, "Yeah, I heard it was the size of Hill's fist."

My mouth dropped. I felt my knees go weak. *The size of the surgeon's fist?!* I thought. *That's half his brain! He really is doomed!*

I stared down at my hand. In a daze, I turned to leave the room. Nobody up to this point had specifically told me that the part of the temporal lobe that had been removed was five or five and a half centimeters—a critical amount, but hardly in the fist range. I stumbled across the street to my room and slumped down onto the bed.

I took off my shoes and socks as unanswerable questions reeled through my mind. *What will ever become of David? Am I crazy to keep pushing for his recovery? Is he just going to keep lying there the rest of his life? Oh, God,* I prayed, *where do we go from here? This is awful!*

Maybe a little hot chocolate on this chilly night would calm my churning mind. I walked down the hall to the hospice's common area, where refreshments could be prepared. I made my cocoa and headed back to my room—only to realize I had locked myself out! I had left the room key inside on the dresser.

Now what could I do? I began searching the building for a caretaker of some kind. Nobody was in sight. I called for help. Nobody answered.

I realized I had no choice but to head across the street coatless and with my bare feet to the hospital. Soon I was shivering as badly as David on his ice blanket. I ran up to the first nurse I saw and said, "Can you help me find another key to my room over at the hospice? I locked myself out, and I'm so upset—I'm freezing to death!" She naturally had no idea where to find a spare key. But with some phoning she managed to solve my crisis.

That was one of the worst nights of my life. All alone back in my room, I eventually got warm again. But nothing could melt the ice around my heart regarding David. His future looked absolutely bleak. I tossed and turned on my bed throughout the night.

Back at the hospital the next day, I tried to put on a brave face. Inwardly, I was spent. The Lord must have known my desperate state, because I was walking down a corridor at one point when I looked up—and suddenly, no more than fifteen feet in front of me, was Shari Krause, one of my dearest friends from Yakima! I had trained her at Penney's for my position when I left.

"What are *you* doing here?!" I cried.

"I drove over to spend some time with you," she replied. "I thought you could use some company."

Could I ever! In one of the lowest troughs of my life, here was a friend to lift me up. We hugged each other and began talking. Soon I took her in to see David, whom she knew from the store. We spent hours trying to get him to recognize Shari, to no avail.

As the afternoon drew to a close, she had an idea. "Let me take you out to dinner."

"I can't," I replied.

"Why not?"

"I really have to be here. David might need me."

Shari said, "Well, I'm sure you can leave for just an hour or so."

"No, really—if something happened, I'd feel so bad," I replied. My separation anxiety was intense.

"Leone, listen to me," she retorted. "You need to get away from here once in a while. I *insist* on taking you to dinner. You can call back while we're out, if you really think you need to."

"Well—okay, if I can call, like, every fifteen minutes or so." I know that sounds totally neurotic. But in my state, it felt like a necessity.

We did go out to a restaurant for a nice dinner. I called several times. The nurse told me each time that David was the same and that I should go ahead and enjoy my meal. In fact, I did. I came back to the hospital that evening in a much improved frame of mind.

I'm so grateful for what Shari did that day and continued to do in the weeks and months to come. She was one of a legion of support people who held me up when I was fragile and about to collapse.

First Rehab

The only flickers of good news were that as the week wore on, David's temperature problem subsided and the chest infection was controlled. His brain pressure stabilized to the point that the monitor could be removed. Best of all, he was able to be weaned off the respirator. By the next Monday, November 4, we were informed that he could be moved out of the ICU to St. Joseph's small rehabilitation unit.

There, physical therapists bravely began trying to see what they could do with him. I'll never forget watching two of them try to get him into a sitting position. It was like trying to lift the *Titanic* off the bed. He was absolutely limp.

They resorted to the trick of tucking an ice bag under the back of his neck to see if that would jolt him into rising up. No such luck. They backed away, realizing that they were torturing him more than anything else. With tears in their eyes, they looked at each other and tried to think what to try next.

Yet they recognized something unusual about this paralyzed young patient. At least three different staff members told me something along the lines of "You know, he has a peaceful spirit about him. We have to keep trying to get through to him." One young man looked directly in my eyes and said, "Thank God you're here. Thank God that you're a mother and you're right here with us. When a patient doesn't have a supporting family around him, we can accomplish so much less."

"Yes, we're with you all the way," I answered. "We love him, and we're not going to give up."

Bud and Lori would come back to Lewiston from time to time, although their work in Yakima was calling. One day Bud took on the onerous task of driving up to Pullman and cleaning out David's off-campus room. This also included finding a tow bar and pulling the infamous Triumph sports car back to Yakima.

The police had already visited David's room as part of their accident investigation, talking to David's roommate and picking up additional details. They told us they had greatly revised their initial assumption about our son. In the beginning they knew he was a college student, and WSU had a reputation as a party school. So when a motorcycle-riding WSU junior had wiped out on the highway, they had naturally looked at each other and nodded. He fit the stereotype.

Then they walked into his room! Everything was in good order. His bed was nicely made, with a little quilt I had made him long ago on top, decorated with boyish-looking trains. His Bible sat prominently on his desk. The room was neat and clean. Maybe this fellow wasn't such a daredevil after all, they concluded.

Somewhere in this time period—I can't recall when—Leo, my ex-husband, arrived from his home in Alaska to visit his son. This put the rest of the family on edge. Even David, who was not reacting to much stimulus at all, evidenced increased agitation whenever Leo came to his bedside; his blood pressure would go up. The hospital staff asked him to keep his visits very short.

Little was said between Leo and me. A day or so later, Leo got back on the plane to go home again.

On Thursday, November 9, another EEG was taken. The

brain activity was still extremely low. The written report termed it "a markedly abnormal recording. There is evidence of diffuse cerebral dysfunction and suppression of activity. . . . In comparison with the previous recording of 11-01-89 there has been no significant change."

The Feeding Tube

Another blow landed the next Monday morning, November 13. That was the day when the doctors said that David simply wasn't getting enough nutrition through his nasal tube, which had been in place since the beginning. His nose passageway was getting irritated, and he was also having reflux problems in his esophagus.

"He obviously can't swallow food by mouth," Dr. Moreno remarked, "and the nose tube just isn't going to work long-term. The only alternative is to put a feeding tube into his stomach."

I cringed inside. It sounded so permanent. My hopes that he would someday eat on his own were being dashed.

"Do you really think it's necessary?" I pleaded.

"Yes, I do," he replied. "It is our only reasonable alternative in order to keep feeding him. Here is the consent form for you to sign."

My hand quivered as I reached for the pen. They would be putting a hole into David's abdomen and securing a foreign object inside him for who knew how long. I felt trapped. I didn't want to do this—but what else could I say? I finally wrote my name on the line.

When I told Dale about it that night on the phone, he was calm. The logic of the procedure made sense to him, even though it wasn't something either of us wanted. It felt good to at least be able to talk this through with him. He was such an anchor for my spirit.

Meanwhile, Dale kept quiet about things I didn't need to hear. For example, when he had returned to his job in Hawaii and described the terrible ordeal to his construction crew, the reaction was interesting. Knowing Dale was a stepfather, more than one guy said, "Boy, that's tough. Bet you won't be sticking around for *that* kind of a deal, will ya?" They fully expected what happens all too often in blended families when hardship strikes: The nonblood parent starts looking for the exit.

"I'm not going anywhere," Dale told his workers. "They need me more than ever now."

What some of them didn't know was that my husband had already been through the shock of losing a son. One night back in 1984, Rick Nunley, the second of his four boys, had fallen asleep at the wheel of his tractor-trailer rig on an Idaho highway and was killed instantly. Dale never even had a chance to say good-bye. Now another young man in the family was in a life-and-death situation. Dale would fight with every ounce of strength and every resource he had to avoid a second funeral.

Words cannot express how much Dale's love and commitment have meant to me throughout this entire journey. This man deserves a medal. He has worked and prayed and planned beside me every step of the way.

Once the feeding tube was in place, David's condition continued to plateau. I began talking with Dr. Hill and the other doctors about whether he could be moved to a Yakima hospital so we could put at least some of our life back together. Dale would bring Bill and young Steve back at their Christmas break, then start easing himself out of the Hawaii construction project. The Yakima construction company certainly needed Dale's attention once again anyway.

"Yes, we think that's a feasible plan," the Lewiston doctors replied. "If you can line up a medical team there to take over the case, we will authorize his discharge and transfer. He'll have to make the trip by ambulance, obviously."

I got to work making phone calls. Through the church I secured Dr. Roger Bracchi to serve as David's main physician. A family practitioner, he and his wife, Lori, had even served as youth group sponsors when my older sons were teenagers. He made the necessary arrangements with a neurosurgeon, Dr. Leslie Bornfleth, and others.

By Friday, November 17, we were preparing for the big expedition. Bud was back in Lewiston to help. I think he was shocked to see how much weight David had lost over the past weeks. Soon we said farewell and many thanks to the people at St. Joseph. These nurses had been just incredible. I told them how much I appreciated their service and their willingness to keep me informed. I gave Dr. Hill our fervent gratitude.

As the gurney was wheeled into the ambulance, I was given a massive file of medical documentation to hand-carry to the new set of doctors. Climbing into the front right seat, I began browsing through the stack. In his discharge summary, Dr. Hill had written a poignant paragraph:

> EEGs showed severe cortical dysfunction, and Dr. Stockard felt that, based on the EEG, [David] was unlikely to wake up. This was reviewed with the family, and they

are very uncomfortable with that statement. [*To say the least!*] I discussed with them the fact that he has not made significant progress. They feel that almost any little motion is a sign of improvement and are still hopeful that he will awaken and participate in rehabilitation. I have told them that if he did not show any signs of improvement by six to eight weeks, then I thought that he should be placed in an extended care facility [i.e., a nursing home].

With my heart a jumble of hope and uncertainty, we slowly pulled out of Lewiston. The ambulance was quiet. I told myself that even though David was terribly damaged, he was still with me, and for that I could be grateful. We headed west along the Snake River and began the half-day trip across the Washington prairie.

FOUR

"Not Another Dollar"

It was dark when we pulled up to St. Elizabeth
Medical Center in Yakima, and both the ambulance driver and I knew David was in worse shape
after the trip. The instant I touched him, even
before he was wheeled into the building, I could
tell he was burning up with fever again. His face
was flushed, his eyes remained closed, and his
breathing was short and labored, almost to the
point of panting.

The nursing staff quickly transferred him to a
fifth-floor bed, while at a glass-enclosed desk Dr.
Bracchi began working through page after page after
page of the thick stack of records and reports I had
brought him. I watched from the other side of the
room and felt sorry for him at this late hour. No
doubt he had already seen dozens of patients over

the course of a long day. Now I was loading onto his shoulders an incredibly complicated, nearly hopeless case.

A slender man with dark hair, he read for at least twenty minutes before turning to speak with the nurses. Eventually, he came over to sit beside me. "Well, his temperature has spiked up to 104 degrees orally," he began in his soft-spoken, understated manner, "which means the pneumonia he was battling in Lewiston has resurged. We will of course treat it aggressively with antibiotics. We need to get on top of this as quickly as possible.

"This being Friday night, I won't be able to get Dr. Bornfleth and the other specialists to examine him until Monday morning. But I will put in the requests for consultation."

Dr. Bracchi covered some other medical information, then paused before broaching a particularly sensitive subject.

"Leone," he finally continued, "we need to talk about a decision regarding life support. As we move forward through the coming days and weeks . . . if, for example, David's heart were to stop, what would you want us to do?" He wasn't pushing me in any particular direction. He was simply, in his thorough way, preparing for all eventualities.

I didn't know what to say. "Well, uh," I stammered, "I guess I don't know." And then I reverted to the same question I had asked Dr. Hill back in Lewiston a month before. "What would you do if this were your son?"

Dr. Bracchi shook his head. "I can't even imagine being in this position," he admitted. "So I don't think I could say what I would decide if I were in your shoes."

"Surely you can tell me something," I persisted.

He thought for another moment, then said, "Personally

speaking, I would not want to live the way it looks like David is going to be. But don't get me wrong; I will still treat him as aggressively as I can."

I gave myself time to reason silently as well. Then I said, "Okay. If his heart quits, or if he stops breathing for some reason, we won't go through heroic measures to bring him back. No heart massages or emergency codes and all that. Just let him be. The Lord can determine whether he revives or not."

Dr. Bracchi nodded silently and looked down to write a note. He then stood up, finishing the conversation for now. His final words made a deep impression on me. "Please pray for me as I begin to treat David."

With that, he walked away, leaving me grateful for the service of a medical professional who knew how much he needed divine assistance.

On the Edge

I had no home to call my own for the time being; renters still occupied our house on Bristol Way. We had given them notice that we would need to terminate the agreement at the end of the month so we could move back in. But for the next two weeks of November, including the Thanksgiving holiday, I'd be camping out at Bud and Lori's small apartment in the rough part of town where they ministered to drug abusers and other people in need.

To be honest, you could say I was "doing drugs" myself— that is, I was taking Restoril, a sleep medication the doctors had given me in Lewiston to try to help calm my agitation and give me some rest. The stuff was powerful enough that sometimes I would be unaware even while walking around in the middle of the night. The medication also made me ravenously hungry. My precious daughter-in-law, Lori, had begun making Christmas cookies in advance, and they mysteriously began disappearing! The culprit turned out to be me—there were crumbs in my bed to prove it. I had no idea I was scarfing down her handiwork during the early hours, but I couldn't deny the evidence. There were Ritz crackers and M&M's as well. Bud and Lori both laughed and said they'd have to hide the goodies from now on.

Nearly every waking moment, of course, I was back at St. Elizabeth (known today as Yakima Regional Medical Center). Friends began to pour in as well, now that David was nearby. They were jolted by what they saw. Joy Campbell, a longtime friend who had been in a weekly prayer partnership with another woman and me throughout the early 1980s, told me later about her first reaction. "He was kinked up in a Z shape, looking totally out of it. My first thought was, *He's going to die, and that's probably the best thing.* But I said nothing to you, of course. It was all I could do to stay steady in your presence. I couldn't be positive, and I didn't want to be negative. I tried to just stay on a 'low hum,' I guess."

This was the woman who remembered David as the practical joker in her Sunday school class a decade before, the "monkey" who would never sit still, she said. A former special education teacher, Joy was knowledgeable of what could be accomplished with mentally challenged students. But this present situation seemed completely beyond hope.

A coworker from JCPenney, Weed Schilperoort, came with her husband. She said later, "We just couldn't imagine him living." They, too, kept their dire predictions to themselves and tried simply to be my comfort. She still has an expensive leather jacket that bears my tearstains on the shoulder.

On Monday, November 20, I met Dr. Leslie Bornfleth, the neurosurgeon, for the first time. A man of small stature, he was impeccably dressed and very articulate. He said he was impressed with the work that his counterpart, Dr. Hill, had done in Lewiston. However, he was also realistic about the future. In his consultation report he wrote that "the head is normal" and "the incision is well healed" but went on to write:

> The patient is deeply comatose, not following commands, not reacting to noxious [or irritating, such as a pinprick] stimulation. . . . The patient had an EEG which showed diffuse severe dysrhythmia [abnormal brain wave patterns]. This makes the prognosis very poor. There is nothing specific to be done from the neurological standpoint.

In other words, don't expect brain surgery to accomplish anything further. Dr. Bornfleth also wrote that, looking back to October 15, he suspected David's brain had been significantly deprived of oxygen at the time of the accident.

A few days later, he ran his own EEG so he could examine the results firsthand. He reviewed the statistics with me, and again, the prospects were grim. At the end of our talk, he added, "There is, however, a slight—*and I do mean slight*—improvement over the findings of the Lewiston brain tests." My ears perked up, because this was not a man to speak loosely in any way. He always chose his words with great precision. "I would not say this if I didn't think so, but there may be some hope here."

For the first time, a physician had expressed more than gloom and doom for David. I clung to his words, memorizing them. Of course, none of this would matter if we lost the battle with pneumonia.

A pulmonary specialist, Dr. Greenberg, had been hard at work on that from the beginning. He found it to be actually worse than pneumonia: David also showed the complication of empyema on the right side, where the infection had spread into the space between the lungs and the chest wall. The doctors were battling more than just fluid; a thick mucus was building up there.

Chest tubes were inserted once again between the ribs, although the infection proved too muddy to be easily drained off. Meanwhile, broad-spectrum antibiotics were thrown into the fray. David's temperature continued to sizzle. His only motion was an occasional yawn.

This battle raged throughout the Thanksgiving holiday and on into the next week. At least one doctor on the case raised the option of surgically opening up the chest cavity to scrape out the infection, since chest tubes apparently were not going to get the job done. But would David even survive such a shock to the system? "That's a fair question," the doctors honestly replied. "We would definitely be taking a risk."

"I really don't want to hurt him any worse than he's already been damaged," I said.

They agreed that they would wait to operate until Friday, December 1. In the meantime, we would all keep hoping that the chest tubes would start doing at least a little good. The temperature reports continued in the 104 to 105 degree range. Day after day, I would sit by his bed watching him struggle for breath and, at the same time, shiver in response to the ice blankets that were there to cool him down.

Pastor Wayne Pickens asked me one day, "Would you be interested in having the elders of the church come for an anointing prayer, like it says in the New Testament? How would you feel about that?"

"Absolutely," I replied. "He was anointed with oil back in Lewiston, but I would certainly welcome it again."

At 7:00 Thursday morning, November 30, before the various men went to work, they gathered at St. Elizabeth. Pastor Wayne and twelve elders surrounded David's bed. After the application of oil to his forehead, they pleaded with God to intervene in this desperate situation. They asked for his pneumonia and empyema to recede and for him to regain consciousness.

When they finished, I thanked them for caring enough to come by as a group. They left, and I continued my vigil.

That evening, the nurse who took David's temperature smiled as she said, "Well, it's actually down just a fraction." I forget the actual decimal point, but the fever was starting to break. This was the first relief we had seen since arriving from Lewiston nearly two weeks before. My heart swelled with a tiny glimmer of hope.

When the doctors arrived the next morning, they decided to call off the planned surgery, at least for the time being. David would not have to go under the knife again after all.

In the following days, the trend continued. God's healing touch plus the powerful antibiotics beat back the infection, and David's chest gradually cleared. Late one night after I had left, a nurse was gently stroking David's face with her hand. Feeling the stubble, she commented, "Your mama's going to have to shave you pretty soon."

Without warning, a sound arose from the patient in the bed. Out came a clear one-word query: "Mama?"

The nurse bolted upright and then nearly fainted. "Yes, your mama! That's right!" she cried. "Say it again, David: *Mama. Mama.*"

He would not. She went running out of the room to tell the other nurses of the miracle that had just occurred. This dreadfully brain-damaged young man had actually uttered his first word.

When I arrived the next morning, the ward was abuzz. "He said your name last night!" they chorused. "He actually said 'Mama!'"

I was overjoyed, as were they. "Try to get him to say it again," they urged. I went straight to my son and began pleading with all my might for a repeat performance. I got no response at all. But my hopes were buoyed by this simple, if fleeting, breakthrough from the silent prison.

By the middle of December, the medical team classified David's overall health as stable. Not that this meant he was normal by any stretch of the imagination; his brain injury was still as profound as ever, leaving him nearly unresponsive to the world around him. But at least he was no longer "sick" in the medical definition of the term.

The Napkin

By now the renters had moved out, and I busied myself with putting our house back together. Rick Dieker headed up a team of five men from our church who came to help me pull our belongings out of storage and get them back under our roof. Fueled by the Restoril sleep aid, I plunged into a frenzy of getting things in place. Within forty-eight hours I even had pictures hung and some new wallpapering done. One morning I discovered that during the night I had muscled the heavy eight-foot dining room table aside, spread out an Oriental rug, then moved the table into place on top of the rug and positioned the chairs around perfectly—all alone! That was the point when I decided I'd better stop taking the medication before I did something really bizarre.

Christmas decorations that season, however, were minimal. But Dale and the two boys would be arriving December 23 from Hawaii, and I wanted the place to look halfway festive. I thought of little Steve, just seven years old, and knew I had to make an attempt at holiday fun. But none of us were exactly in a celebrative mood.

When they got off the plane, I gave each of them a hug, and we headed straight to the hospital. Bill remembers indelibly his first view of his older brother, his hero in many ways. David had been a successful wrestler, and Bill had tried to follow in his steps. Now, as we stepped off the elevator on the fifth floor, there was David in a wheelchair, slumped over and drooling.

Fifteen-year-old Bill went into slow motion as he walked in David's direction. Getting down on one knee, he put his hand carefully on David's back and said, "Hey, man—we're finally home. We just got off the plane. We came to see you."

David might as well have been deaf and blind.

Tears filled my eyes as I watched Bill stagger emotionally under the enormity of what had happened. Until now, he and

Steve had only heard our secondhand reports of their brother's condition. Now they were facing it in all its tragedy.

"David, sit up straight, okay?" Bill admonished. "Come on, man—you gotta get up." Again, there was no response from David's limbs, no flicker in his eyes. It was a case, as the saying goes, of the lights being on but nobody being home. Bill looked at me with a pathetic numbness.

We were each coming to terms in our own way with the harsh reality of what a head injury does to a family. There would be no going back to previous times. The future would be massively different. Not a single day or week, not a single plan or dream would go untouched. Nothing lay beyond the gravitational pull of David's vast set of needs.

That evening at home, the four of us tried to decorate the Christmas tree. It was miserable. Our hearts were not in the task. We plodded onward and then fell into bed, exhausted.

On Christmas morning we arranged to bring David home for the day in the hospital's special van, which had a lift for his wheelchair. The nurses gave us instructions on how to feed him Ensure through his feeding tube, change his diaper, and transfer him safely from place to place. We weren't brave enough to try keeping him overnight, to be sure. But for the holiday, we wanted to give him a taste of home.

We fumbled our way through the gift-opening time. It felt strange to us all. We missed Rob, who was still at sea with the navy. The peace and joy of Christmas were far from our senses. What could we possibly reach for on the horizon?

And then, late in the day, shortly before taking him back to the hospital, another tiny blip of encouragement came silently into our lives.

The house was full of family members as we shared a meal together. Bud was trying out the video camera we had gotten a few months earlier, catching one person after another with food in their mouths. Eventually he put the camera on a tripod and simply left it running.

By now we were getting more into the habit of talking normally to David, pretending he could understand even though we assumed he couldn't. On this afternoon, he was drooling as usual as he sat in his wheelchair. A napkin had been placed in his lap. "David, use your napkin to wipe your mouth," somebody said.

"Yeah, David—see if you can wipe your mouth, okay?" somebody else repeated.

His left hand—the more active of the two—wandered aimlessly. He made no sound or acknowledgment. But suddenly Bud cried, "Look! He's trying to do it!" Ever so clumsily, David was lifting the napkin in the direction of his lips.

We held our breath. In time, after further meandering in the air, he brushed his mouth with the napkin. *He actually understood what we said! He comprehended a directive and responded to it.*

A wave of hope rushed over me in that moment. "David, you did it!" I cried as I hugged him. "You knew what we wanted you to do, and you got it done!"

We asked him to repeat the motion. This time he stared at us blankly. His hand remained motionless. This would not be a sudden breakthrough.

But there was no denying that at least once he had heard and processed information. We had the videotape to prove it.

I could not wait to tell Dr. Bracchi the next day. He smiled and nodded. "That's good, Leone. But we still have an awfully long way to go, you know."

Yes, I knew. I expected a cautious physician to say something like that. Inside my mother heart, however, I was singing.

What's Next?

The holidays gave our many friends more opportunities to visit David, since they had extra time off work. A steady parade of visitors showed up at the hospital. Sometimes it seemed as if there were twenty people in his room at once. Everybody held fantasies of being the one who would suddenly snap David back to full awareness.

"Is he getting too much company?" I asked Dr. Bracchi one day. "Given his mental and physical condition, are we overwhelming him with too much stimulation?"

He shook his head as he replied, "The truth is, if David has a chance at all, these people are his best chance." He welcomed all the attention that familiar faces from the past could provide.

Their presence gave me a lift as well, especially in the absence of Dale, who had to fly back to Hawaii to complete his construction project there. Jacquie Wonner, a woman from our church who had served as a volunteer alongside David in some outreaches, came by. She worked in the health care field and knew to watch for small signals. She noticed that David seemed to prefer looking toward the window, where the light was.

Taking his hand, she talked to him for a while, trying to reestablish herself in his mind. Then she said, "David, if you can feel me holding your hand, squeeze it, okay?"

One little finger seemed to push against her hand ever so gently.

Next we began experimenting with his sense of smell. Dill pickles have always been an obsession in our family. One day as David lay in bed, I brought out a dill pickle and waved it under his nose. His head came right up off the pillow!

A little later, we tried doing the same with a stick of chewing gum. Lo and behold, he snapped at it with his mouth and bit off a piece! We gasped with surprise. Of course, we knew we had to get the piece out of his mouth before he choked on it.

"David, that's wonderful!" I said. "But give me back the gum now."

His jaws stayed tightly clenched.

I called for a nurse to help. "He's got a piece of gum in his mouth! I wanted to see if he'd recognize the smell, and he bit off a little bit."

She had no better results than I at retrieving the gum. Before it was all over, three nurses were required—one on each side holding down his arms, and a third up in the bed on her knees forcing him to open his mouth. What a scene I had created. But they forgave me, because they were equally pleased that he was reacting to stimuli.

Little things such as these made for lively storytelling. But as we moved into January and the decision makers all returned from their holiday vacations, it became clear that medical opinion was at a crossroads. What should be done with David now that, technically speaking, he had no more "illness" to treat? We, of course, wanted him moved into St. Elizabeth's rehabilitation unit to see what further progress could be gained.

The head of that unit was a somewhat crusty woman in her late forties or early fifties whom I shall call Dr. Smith. As Yakima's only practicing physiatrist (an MD who specializes in physical therapy), she held his fate in her hands. If she found him a candidate for treatment, he would be accepted. If she felt he was unlikely to improve, he would be sent out the door. We had heard that her bedside manner was, shall we say, less than gentle.

A nurse and I were in David's room just casually talking to him one morning when Dr. Smith marched in to conduct her assessment.

"David, close your eyes," she ordered with all the finesse of a marine sergeant.

David stared into space, motionless.

"David, stick out your tongue," she commanded next.

He had never done this particular motion since his accident, and he wasn't about to start now.

She tried a few more directives, all of which failed to elicit a proper response. I honestly think David was afraid of her.

Turning to her assistant, she snapped, "Start finding a nursing home for this patient."

"Why?" I cried. "Isn't that a little hasty? You've only seen him for a minute or so. He's been doing at least a few things we've asked him to do. We had him home for Christmas, and he picked up a napkin—"

"Look," she interrupted, "you can see for yourself. He's never going to be functional the rest of his life. This is a major head injury, the cortex is destroyed, the left temporal lobe has been greatly excised—it's over. We can't just maintain people like this in a working hospital. That's what nursing homes are for."

I was shocked at her bluntness, especially right in front of David. This woman was getting under my skin, even if she was a doctor.

"Well, before I give in to that," I retorted, "I'll take him home and give him therapy myself. I'm not giving up that easily, even if you are."

Her eyes narrowed as she looked at me. "Let me tell you what you're saying," she said. "Number one, you cannot take care of him medically. You don't know how to manage a feeding tube or any of the other complications of this case.

"Number two, your family will fall apart. I've seen it happen over and over. People think they can do the impossible at home, and before they know it, their marriage is gone and their other kids are alienated.

"Number three, you will lose every social relationship in your life. Your friends will drop you in an instant. In the end, you will be stuck all alone with this person for the rest of your life.

"So if you know what's good for you, take my advice—especially if you have other children in the family. I wouldn't jeopardize my home or my finances; in fact, I wouldn't put one more dollar into this boy."

With that, she stormed out of the room.

A flood of tears welled up within me, and I didn't want David to see me break down. I ran from the room and caught a waiting elevator. On the ground floor, I emerged into the main lobby, my mind still reeling from the encounter. I could hardly breathe.

"Leone!" a woman's voice called out. "Over here!"

I turned toward the sound. To my amazement, there stood Kathy Perrigo, the director of children's ministries at our church, along with her husband, Larry. A gracious and mature couple, they had come to visit at just the critical hour. Kathy and I sat down on a large couch together, and I buried my head into her shoulder as the sobs exploded from deep within me. She held me close as I wept for a long time.

Many minutes later I calmed down enough to explain why I was so distraught. "The main doctor from rehab just came up to David's room to evaluate him. She said he's a hopeless case and will be sent to a nursing home," I gasped.

"Oh, Leone, I'm so sorry!" Kathy replied.

"I tried to tell her I'd take care of him myself if I had to, and she basically told me I was an idiot. Not in so many words, but that was the main drift." I dissolved in a new rush of tears. I closed my eyes and burrowed into Kathy's shoulder again.

We sat there for hours, it seemed, grieving the brusque declaration and, even more, the loss of hope. Kathy prayed quietly with me, that the Lord would come and soothe my spirit, giving me courage to face the future and wisdom to know what to try next.

Reprieve

The next morning I dragged myself back to the hospital, fearing the worst. I was sure I would be confronted by authorities with papers for me to sign, discharging David to a bleak future.

When I got to the fifth floor, a nurse greeted me with a big smile on her face. "Guess what? Good news!" she said. "David woke up with a bladder infection this morning!"

"So—why is that good news?" I queried.

"That means he doesn't have to leave our floor just yet!" she bubbled. "He has an illness, and we'll just have to keep taking care of him until it goes away."

A faint smile crossed my face. What an odd turn of events.

The sentence Dr. Smith had passed down would at least be postponed. I didn't know how things were going to work out, but at least we had some additional time to think and plan.

David fought off the infection throughout January, and he was healthy enough that one Sunday we got permission to take him in our car to church. He was sitting up more now and was becoming a little more flexible in his joints. With considerable effort we wheeled him into the sanctuary and parked him beside us in a row near the back.

He was still not alert. The spacey look in his eyes told us he wasn't connecting with most of his surroundings. We could only hope that this familiar place and the familiar sounds would touch a chord somewhere inside him.

The music began, and eventually we progressed to the other parts of the service. I was moved with a sense of God's peace and loving care for us in the midst of our trial. Then Pastor Wayne stood up and said, "I see that we have someone very special in our service today. I want to make sure you all know who's here." With that, he came down from the pulpit and began walking up the aisle in our direction.

"David McRae has come back here to West Side," he announced, as heads turned all over the sanctuary. "We've been praying much for this young man, and today he's here in our midst once again. I think we should all join together as a group asking God to bless him and heal him."

He placed his hand on David's head and began to pray the most wonderful prayer. "Lord, we are so glad as a congregation to see David with us once again. We ask you to especially bless him today. Bless his family for making the effort to bring him. Let your healing grace continue to expand with great benefit in his life. We welcome him into our arms today, just as you have held him ever since the accident. . . ." I don't remember what else he prayed; my emotions were overflowing. I do recall that when he finished, Pastor Wayne bent down and gave our son a gentle kiss on the forehead.

"David, it's good to see you back," he said with a warm smile. He then returned to the pulpit to begin his sermon, as people all over the building reached for their handkerchiefs.

Here in this island of love and care, I took a deep breath. This congregation was our home, our well of strength in the face of discouragement and perplexity. God and his people would bear us up against the headwinds. Whatever the future held for David and for us, we were not alone.

FIVE

End of the Medical Line?

The rest of January 1990 turned into a crusade to disprove Dr. Smith's gloomy assessment. The fifth-floor nurses were as motivated as I was to get David to respond—and to document it on video. While the antibiotics were working on his bladder infection, we tried everything we could think of to stimulate his mind.

The evidence began to grow. We'd put a scarf over his head, for example, and tell him to pull it off. His left hand would eventually find the cloth and remove it. (Since the brain's hemispheres control the opposite sides of the body, David's right hand was—and still is—less agile due to the surgery on the left temporal lobe. His left hand is able to accomplish more.)

We got David to pick up a ball. Soon after that,

he would even place the ball into a bowl for us. He also managed to twist a cap onto a bottle, again left-handed. Everything was videotaped.

He still was not speaking, however, and he frequently could not repeat an action he had successfully done once. "Do it again, David," we'd plead, but the result would be nothing. To look into his face was to sense that he was clawing through a maze of cotton. Sometimes he could see what you were trying to say; ten minutes later he'd get nothing but a white blur.

But I wasn't going to give up, and neither was the nursing staff. They had their own rather choice opinions about Dr. Smith, gained from past experience. I still remember one nurse, a tall blond, who exclaimed, "If she tries to take him out of here, I'll throw myself across the door!" They desperately wanted to prove the expert wrong.

Another nurse named Pauline was kind enough to keep me going with food. She could tell I wasn't paying attention to my own nutrition; she'd catch me coming in with a brown bag with nothing more than a carrot or a piece of cheese in it. "Leone," she would say, "here's an extra lunch tray we had left over. Why don't you take it? Otherwise I'll just have to throw it out." This happened more than once.

Late each afternoon I'd drive home to fix dinner for my other two boys, then return for a couple of hours in the evening. Dale was still in Hawaii, trying to wrap up his construction duties. I felt bad about leaving Bill in charge of young Steve each night, having him get Steve to bed—but I couldn't tear myself away from David's side. I was a mom with too many balls to juggle all at once.

When I finally climbed into bed myself around eleven

o'clock, I'd pick up my "rehab bible," as I called it: a sixty-page booklet entitled *Traumatic Brain Injury: A Guide for the Patient and Family.*[2] I read it over and over, night after night, immersing myself in the physiology of the brain and the ten steps back from trauma, starting with "coma" and ending at "normal." This became my road map of hope.

As the month came to an end, we bombarded Dr. Smith with the most persuasive case we could, supported by the videotapes we had created. We had her cornered, it seemed. She wasn't happy about it, but in the end she did admit David to the rehabilitation department on the first floor to see what might be accomplished. We viewed this as a huge victory.

His room there was small and dull, with no color accents anywhere. His only window looked out onto a flat rooftop. But the rehab staff fell in love with him just as enthusiastically as the previous group of nurses had. The physical therapists and occupational therapists went to work.

Cara Anderson, his nursing case manager, was especially attentive and hopeful. I directed her attention to the possibility of his eating more. "Do you think we could try to see about swallowing?" I asked her right away. "I just hate the idea of this feeding tube; the sooner we can get rid of it, the better. We already gave him ice chips upstairs, and then even a Popsicle!" I added with a grin, "I was going to try some pudding until the nurses caught me."

"Well, let's find out what he can do," she replied. "If you give a person a small piece of solid food that's really tart, it can shock them into swallowing it. We'll try a little pineapple and see what happens."

Sure enough, it worked. David got the pineapple bit down.

We all celebrated. Within a few days, he was eating other things as well. This emboldened me all the more.

Friday, February 9, would be his twenty-second birthday. I showed up that afternoon with some ice cream and a tiny piece of cake. I didn't have official permission, but so what? "Happy birthday, David!" I cried. "People ought to eat whatever they want on their birthday." Lo and behold, he eagerly began chewing and swallowing. A smile spread across his face.

Not long after that, Dr. Smith stopped by to see us. By now I had safely gotten the cake plate out of sight. She opened up his medical chart and said, in a surprisingly pleasant tone, "Well, look at this—February 9. It's your birthday, isn't it, David? It's my mother's birthday too. You're an Aquarius just like her." Inside I thought, *If her source of guidance is a horoscope, no wonder I'm not connecting with her!* But I opted to let the comment pass without a response.

On the main issue between us, she remained as unyielding as ever. She had declared David to be in a persistent vegetative state, and nothing was going to change her mind. The rules said that patients could stay in rehab only if they showed meaningful, verifiable progress, and she could see none. That meant Medicaid wouldn't keep paying the bills (our insurance dispute was still pending at this point). So she could get rid of David as soon as the paperwork was completed.

A Distant Sorrow

Sunday, February 25, was a day similar in many ways to those Sundays that had preceded it. I took the boys with me to church, then fed them a quick lunch and hurried back to the hospital by early afternoon. I stayed there for the rest of the

day, driving home in the winter darkness once David was settled for the night.

Unbeknownst to me, however, something happened early
that morning in the opposite corner of the nation that would
mark a family's life as profoundly as David's accident had hit
our own. An apparently healthy young woman, just four years
older than our son, got up around 5:30 a.m. and collapsed with
a thud in the hallway of her St. Petersburg, Florida, apartment.
Her husband, still in bed, heard the noise and came running to
see what had happened. Getting no response from his wife on
the floor, he called her nearby parents and then dialed 911.
Paramedics soon arrived and did their best to revive the young
woman. They were not successful, so she was rushed through
the still-empty streets to a local hospital. There doctors began
to treat her, concluding eventually that she had suffered some
kind of cardiac arrest accompanied by loss of oxygen to the
brain.

Her name was Theresa (Terri) Marie Schiavo.

Hardly anyone heard about this tragedy for years to
come—I certainly didn't. The Florida family went through
their own private travail of fear and uncertainty, trying to figure out what had happened to their beloved family member
and what to do next, even as our family had been doing for
nineteen weeks now. How ironic that both tragedies struck on
a Sunday morning.

Our paths would not cross for many years. Only much later,
as the entire world belatedly focused on Terri's brain condition
and what it signified for the value of human life, did I come to
grasp the similarities between our two ordeals—and the opposite outcomes.

At that moment in early 1990, I was consumed with lobbying for David's needs. "Dr. Bracchi, we can take the feeding tube out now, can't we?" I urged. "He's swallowing really well. The tube just flops around and gets in the way all the time. Let's pull it out."

"I think we should leave it in just a while longer," Dr. Braachi answered. "We don't know everything that's going to develop in the near future. So to be safe, let's keep it in place."

I was disappointed. I resolved to come back to the subject before too long.

I was relieved that neither he nor Dr. Smith was watching the first time I wheeled David outside the hospital for some fresh air. It was a warm spring day in March, and the early flowers had just started to bloom. "Here, David, look at the pretty flowers," I said, picking one to extend toward his hand.

He grasped the stem, looked at it a minute . . . and then began trying to eat it.

My heart sank as I pulled the flower away from his mouth. We hadn't made very much headway, had we? A million ordinary things of life were still foreign to him. Would he ever understand the purpose of a flower, a tree, a telephone, or a stop sign? Was his recovery an impossible dream?

But in my discouraging moments, Cara or one of the others would tell me something that brightened my day. "I took him back to his room last evening," Cara said, "and just for fun, I said, 'Okay, David, what would you like to do? Do you want to watch TV, or are you tired and want to go to sleep? If you want to watch TV, look at the TV; if you want to go to sleep, look at the bed.' And he clearly looked toward the bed!"

She went on to say that a lot of important signals were very subtle; you could miss them if you weren't paying attention. For example, she watched one evening in the dining commons when David was trying to get some food into his mouth using a fork. The food slipped off, leaving him with an empty utensil. "He got this embarrassed look on his face," Cara reported excitedly. "It was like he was processing a thought, *I hope nobody just saw me do something stupid!* He was consciously thinking about what had just occurred."

David had always been what our family called a "goodie hound"—he loved his snacks. Snickers bars were his favorite. One evening Cara took him out in a wheelchair for a ride down the block. They came to a little mom-and-pop convenience store and went inside.

Looking at the array of candy there, Cara said, "Okay, David, I'll buy you something—which kind do you want? Look at the candy bar you want me to buy for you."

David's eyes readily zeroed in on the Snickers bars. He rolled back to the hospital a happy young man.

Cara began inventing more complicated maneuvers. After warming him up with directives to look left and right, and getting correct responses, she would say, "Now close your eyes and keep them closed until I say the word *green*," or some other random signal not related to the concept of opening his eyes.

David would close his eyes and hold them shut. After about ten seconds, he would lower his head and put his hand over his eyes, as if to make sure he didn't slip up and open them by accident. Finally the release signal would come: "Green!" His head would come up with eyes wide open, a look of success on his face.

Such events encouraged us to believe that the wheels were indeed turning inside his brain. He may have lost much of his speech center, but on the other hand, not all was inert or paralyzed there. Certain processing was indeed going on. We just had to convince the powers that be.

Dr. Smith, for reasons I never did hear or comprehend, decided to raise his dosage of Ritalin, a well-known medication that helps ADHD children (and some adults) focus on the task at hand and control their distractions. She cranked him up to twenty milligrams three times a day, then to thirty milligrams three times a day. The reaction was extreme. David began trembling, drooling more profusely, looking all over the room, and moving his head constantly. His agitation was especially pronounced as he raked his left hand through his hair, front to back, over and over again.

Then after a few hours he would drop into a stupor, almost as if asleep. We could talk to him or even push on his arm with our hands, and we'd get no response whatsoever—until the next dosage of Ritalin would send him up the walls again.

"What is going on?" I protested to Dr. Smith. "This is terrible! He's miserable—not at all like he used to be. Something's got to change here."

She wouldn't admit to any error in judgment. But she did dial him back to just five milligrams of Ritalin twice a day, and his previous composure returned.

The next week, however, he caught the flu. Suddenly we were back to battling high temperatures and congestion. We basically lost two weeks of rehabilitation progress to this temporary, but still serious, illness.

Fighting for a Future

By the time the flu was conquered, we were well into the next, far more intense struggle. David had been in St. Elizabeth's rehab unit for more than six weeks, and it became clear that Dr. Smith had had enough. With a stroke of the pen she could declare that progress was inadequate to meet Medicaid standards. She began actively working to gain placement for him in a budget nursing home in the small town of Wapato, a half-hour drive down the valley.

I knew this would be the end of meaningful life for my son. Whatever potential he had for recovery—and at this point I admitted I didn't know how much to hope for—would be forfeited. David would lie in a bed and rot. They would fill up his stomach tube three times a day, change his diaper, give him a bath every so often, and basically leave him to stare into space. Any flicker of recognition or response on his part would fade—or if it happened at all, would go unnoticed.

"No!" I screamed to myself as I drove back and forth to the hospital. "This must not be! I won't stand for it. I won't give up!" I knew the medical bureaucracy was powerful, but I simply refused to let my son slip away.

What was the alternative? We certainly didn't have the money to pay for his care on our own. The only other choice was to bring him home.

As I thought about it, I recognized that at the moment of childbirth, God had given me the wondrous gift of a life to love, cherish, and nurture. It was the most precious gift imaginable. Was I now going to bail out of that nurturing work when my son needed it most? I could not.

Of course, this would drastically affect the other three

members of my household. I couldn't just pronounce a verdict all by myself. I called for a family meeting to sort this out. Thankfully, Dale had returned from his Hawaii job by now so he could participate in the discussion.

"You know, we're at a crossroads here," I began. "They're going to kick David out of rehab, and we can't stop them. The only choice I can see is to bring him home. I know you may have different feelings about that, and I don't blame you for how you're feeling. But I know there's just no way I can leave him in a nursing home for the rest of his life. I can't do it."

Bill, my teenager, spoke up. "Well, it's not that we don't love David. We all really do. But it's just that—how are we going to handle him? He's totally paralyzed. He can't speak. He can't go to the bathroom on his own. We don't have a shower downstairs for him to use—only that little half bath off the hallway, about the size of a closet. How are we going to keep him clean? I mean, we're not a hospital."

His facts were entirely correct. I knew I was skating on thin ice as I replied, "You're right, Son. It's going to be hard, I know. When it's bath time, I'll probably be asking you to help me drag him up the stairs. It's going to affect all our lives. But we can keep working with him and stretching him and loving him, and who knows what we might be able to accomplish?"

I don't remember what Dale said that day, and of course Steve was too little to voice much of an opinion. Nobody dug in his heels against the idea; we were all just somber as we counted the cost. In the end, we agreed we had to go for it. None of us could swallow the thought of leaving him with less than the best. We had to show our love for David. We had to do what families do.

Before the transfer actually happened, however, a wonderful intervention occurred entirely on its own. Cara Anderson, the rehab nurse, was thinking and worrying about David's future every bit as much as we were. It rankled her to imagine him being shunted off, warehoused in an institution. She knew firsthand the small signals of progress he had evidenced. She believed that continued love and hard work could achieve even more.

Late one evening, at the end of her shift, she drove across town to Dr. Bracchi's office, where he was seeing patients. Walking up to the receptionist in her nurse's uniform, she said, "I'm Cara Anderson from the rehab unit at St. Elizabeth. I don't have an appointment, but I need to talk to Dr. Bracchi about a patient. Is it all right if I just wait here until he's open?"

"Well, his schedule is packed right straight through," the receptionist replied, looking down at her chart. "But I suppose if you want to just hang around . . ."

Cara took a seat. The minutes passed, and the waiting room slowly emptied out. Finally, no one else was left.

She and Dr. Bracchi were both tired after a long day as they sat down to talk. "I'm just concerned about what's going to happen with David McRae," she began. "I really do feel for him. There's more going on there than he's been getting credit for." Cara then began telling stories: the Snickers bar, the signaling toward the bed, other things she had observed.

"I honestly believe he needs to be in a rehabilitation unit that's more geared to his needs than we are," she confessed. "This is hard for me to say, but please don't accept our department's conclusions without doing your own independent assessment. If you could just come spend a little time and see for yourself, I would really appreciate it."

Dr. Bracchi looked into the eyes of this nurse and saw a sincerity not to be brushed aside. She didn't have to be doing this. She honestly cared. He nodded. "Okay, I'll stop by later on tomorrow," he promised.

"Thank you, Doctor," she said with relief. "I know it's the right thing to do." With that, she headed out into the night.

The next evening, Cara watched anxiously as Dr. Bracchi came into the ward, entered David's room, and closed the door behind him. She could only hope and pray that David would "perform" at this critical moment.

In fact, he did. We learned later that when Dr. Bracchi asked him to blink his eyes, he blinked. When asked to keep his eyes tightly closed, he squinted them shut and held on.

"That was very good, David," the doctor replied. "Now reach out with your left hand and touch me."

Up came the arm until it made contact with Dr. Bracchi's body.

"Now how about your right hand? Can you touch me with your right hand?"

David thought about that for a moment. The doctor waited. Then David reached across with his *left* hand to pick up his weaker right arm by the wrist and slowly pull it in Dr. Bracchi's direction until it touched the doctor's arm. David had clearly reasoned that in order to accomplish this task, he would need to invent a novel way to compensate.

Thirty minutes passed before the door opened and Dr. Bracchi emerged from the room. Cara Anderson thought she saw tears in his eyes.

Second Opinion

The two of them began to lay plans for getting a review by a second physiatrist. This would mean taking David out of town, since Dr. Smith had no local peers in her specialty. Somehow the name Dr. Vivian Moise at Sacred Heart Medical Center in Spokane, Washington, came up.

This would mean another arduous highway trip of some two hundred miles. None of us looked forward to that.

But we pressed ahead regardless. Dr. Bracchi wrote a letter describing his young patient. He talked about David's ability to do at least some complex reasoning and asked her to assess whether further rehabilitation should be provided. We all knew that if she wrote a positive report, it would open the door to additional Medicaid funding.

The best facility for rehabilitation in our region, we learned, was Good Samaritan Hospital in Puyallup, across the Cascade Range, just at the edge of Tacoma. The logistics of all this seemed a bit overwhelming at first. But for David, we could attempt no less. We looked forward with a glint of hope.

Maybe we had not reached the end of the medical line after all.

SIX

Feeling Our Way

The appointment in Spokane could not be slated until June, we found. We hated to wait that long, but we had no choice. Meanwhile, as D-day (discharge day) approached, I did not insist that David instantly come home for round-the-clock care. That was my goal, of course. But for the short term I approached the administrator of Summitview Manor, Cal Crowell, with a novel proposal: What if David could spend just the nights there? We'd take care of him all day long at home, then bring him to the facility for sleeping so we could get some rest ourselves.

This long-term care facility had never before made such arrangements, but it helped that Cal and his wife, Sharon, were good friends of ours from church. He listened and said yes, they'd try it. Dr. Bracchi signed the necessary paperwork, and the experiment began—much to the surprise of Dr. Smith. But we were not going to settle for mediocre care at any of the facilities she had in mind.

Throughout April and May 1990, the joy—and exhaustion—of caring for David ourselves became a reality. My days were filled with talking to him, loving him, feeding him (by mouth as much as possible), and trying to stretch him both mentally and physically. He would sit in his wheelchair or on a couch in our family room and just watch me as I worked in the open kitchen, chatting to him all the while.

Moving him from place to place, laying him down to change his diaper, getting him in and out of the car—it all gave me a workout. I'm only five foot one and 110 pounds. The amazing thing is that starting from that point until the present day, more than fifteen years later, I've never torqued my back or suffered other damage from all the lifting and pulling. God must have given me a strong spine because he knew I'd need it.

Each evening we drove David to Summitview to sleep and then picked him up again the next morning. One time, though, I got brave enough to try keeping him overnight. He hadn't seemed to be feeling up to par that day, and I thought I'd like to stay close to him.

He slept that night on a twin-size mattress with a plastic cover that we placed on the family room floor, while I curled up on the couch. About one in the morning, the flu hit him with full force. Suddenly I awoke to the sound of David throwing up. I bolted upright to flip on a light.

His face lay in a pool of vomit, and he was helpless to move. "Oh, David!" I cried. "Let me help you!" I jumped down to roll him off the mattress onto the carpet, then ran to get a towel for cleaning up. What a mess it was.

When I finally got him into a clean T-shirt, changed all the bedding, and gave him a clean pillow half an hour later, we settled down to try to sleep again. Lying in the darkness on the couch, I listened as his breathing stabilized to a steady rhythm. *What if he'd been in the nursing home tonight?* I thought. *Would they have heard him in distress down the hall? Would they have gotten to his side to help him before he choked?* I was so glad I could take care of my son that night, just as I had seen him through many an illness when he was three years old, and five and eight and ten. I was once again fulfilling the role of a mom.

I didn't meet his every need, of course. Dale jumped in with full dedication, lifting him along with me, taking him to the toilet for his regular bowel movement, and cleaning him up afterward. Bill would do his best to activate David's mind by doing drills of "Show me my eyes. Now touch my nose. Now touch my ears."

Bud stopped by whenever he could to help out. As the oldest of my sons, he had long been a mainstay, even back in my single-parenting years. Tuesday and Thursday afternoons became regular visiting times for him. He would take David out for a wheelchair ride in the neighborhood or give him a workout on the big blue therapy ball, which was some thirty inches in diameter and helped stretch David's back muscles.

One time while working in our garage, Bud was inspired to see if David could actually be made to stand up. Using rope, he tied him up to a post, securing his knees, midsection, and upper chest. "Look how straight I've got him, Mom!" he called through the door. I came out to see my son indeed on his feet, although hardly in a natural pose. He didn't seem to be in any pain, just perplexed by all the ado.

"Wow, Bud!" I responded. "He's really straight, all right."

Any physical therapist reading this book will shudder, I'm sure. We were such amateurs—we didn't know what we were doing. We had received no training; we were just winging it. But at least we weren't letting him vegetate. We were keeping him plugged in to the world around him, letting him know we loved him every step of the way.

Friends from church and the neighborhood helped us in this sincere, if sometimes naive, quest. Jacquie Wonner stopped by one day and asked if she could take David for a drive in her little Volkswagen Rabbit. They headed up a picturesque road called Scenic Drive that overlooks the city. Jacquie pointed out various tall buildings and tried to engage his mind.

Then came an intriguing response. David's left hand began to reach out toward the steering wheel. In time he actually was able to grasp it lightly.

"David! Do you want to help me drive?" she asked.

His animated face indicated yes.

Coming down off the overlook area, Jacquie headed southbound on First Avenue into a commercial district. Miner's Drive-In, the most popular hamburger place in town, lay ahead.

"David, now whenever you see Miner's, you let me know, okay?" It wasn't mealtime, but she wanted to see if he would at least recognize the spot from his many visits there as a teenager.

Two or three blocks passed. Then David started to point ahead and get excited. Indeed, the Miner's Drive-In sign had just come into view.

"You're right, David!" Jacquie cried. "There it is. You knew how to find it, didn't you?"

Surrender

April was the month when our tussle with our insurance company finally came to a head. Knowing that this was not going to be easy, we had retained a local attorney to press our contention that since they had accepted David in the beginning as a member under our family coverage, they could not bail out now that he was in need. He reminded the original underwriting office in Hawaii that since the insurance company also did business in the state of Washington, they were subject to Washington laws. "Under our law, you have insured David," he wrote, "and if there is any mistake, it is on your part and not on the part of the Nunleys."

Copies of the complaint went to Hawaii's Office of Consumer Protection, which called for an explanation from the insurance company. On April 14 the corporate counsel sent a long-winded reply that basically said, in thick legalese, that they had fulfilled the terms of their service agreement. They insisted they had properly notified Dale's employer, Kamaole Joint Ventures, of David's disenrollment in a timely manner—something nobody could recall or find evidence of.

Even if they had agreed to cover David's expenses, they would have insisted that anything beyond initial emergency care be done in one of their company-affiliated centers—of which there were none in the Yakima area.

"So what do we do?" I said to Dale as all this became clear.

"I doubt we'll get very far with a lawsuit," he replied. "We thought we had David covered, but they insist we

didn't. Maybe the best route now is just to stick with
Medicaid."

I bristled inwardly against that. Even as a single mother, I
had fought with all my might to avoid going on welfare. And I
had succeeded in getting a job that would pay our bills. Now to
have David on Medicaid for life . . . the thought just killed me.

But I had to admit it was our only realistic option. Obviously no new health insurance company was going to accept
David in his present condition.

We told our attorney he could close the file on this case.
We then set about learning what else we needed to know
about Medicaid's rules and procedures. We were thankful that
such a program existed for the uninsured.

Pulling the Tube

Early in May I was back to nagging Dr. Bracchi about the
stomach feeding tube. I really wanted it out. "David's eating
just fine by mouth," I pleaded. "And now that we're doing all
the daytime care, it's really just a pain to have that tube in.
Can't we please get rid of it?"

"Okay, it's been long enough," he replied. "I'll stop by the
house in a day or two and take it out." For a busy doctor to
make a house call was highly unusual, I knew, but Dr. Bracchi's
dedication to our son was something special.

We all got a huge surprise, however, when Dr. Bracchi
stopped by, knelt down beside David on the daybed where he
was resting, started to pull . . . and discovered the tube
wouldn't come out! "This is strange," he said, applying greater
leverage. As mightily as he tugged, it absolutely refused to
release.

"The Lewiston doctor must have secured it on the inside with a special apparatus," he concluded. "Let me find out more about this."

In the end, David had to go back to the hospital on May 7 for a full-scale extraction procedure under general anesthesia. The tube had been secured inside his stomach with a butterfly device, almost as snug as a molly bolt anchor in a wall intended to hold a heavy picture. Dr. Williams, another physician from our church, had to put an endoscope down David's throat and fish out the feeding tube from the upper direction. What an ordeal!

But at least we were rid of it, which made me very happy.

A few days after its removal came Mother's Day. Dale, as usual, made sure each of the boys had a card to give me—even one from David. He managed to prop a pen in David's left hand and coax him into making a few scratches on the inside. It meant the world to me. Back in the winter I had feared I wouldn't even have this son on this Mother's Day. "Thank you, David!" I cried as I opened the card. "This is the most special one you've ever given me." Then all five of us piled into the car and went to Dairy Queen for a family treat.

That next week, we went to see Dr. Bracchi again, and I told him I was thinking of ending the Summitview overnight assistance toward the end of May. He agreed to process the necessary discharge papers. He also prescribed a long leg brace to try to help David bear more weight on his right (weaker) side. David was nowhere close to standing on his own yet, but we wanted to look forward.

We kept making videotapes of daily life at home so we could track any new developments. They're fun to watch now, since they show David responding ever so faintly to questions with a nod of yes or no. We were starting to get a few small smiles out of him as well.

We spread out an oversize checkerboard just to see what he would do. He'd actually attempt to play the game, although not very successfully. We did the same with tic-tac-toe on a large pad of paper. He could actually mark the Xs he wanted to make, and even win.

When we played a familiar Neil Diamond song on the stereo, he would bounce to the rhythm. When we handed him a banana, he recalled that you first had to peel such a thing, and he would attempt to get the peel off.

"That's good, David!" we would cheer. Whatever showed the brain at work got a rousing approval from the rest of us.

One day I was sitting in the kitchen chatting with my longtime friend Joy Campbell. We were recalling days past when young Rob and David were in the Sunday school department she supervised, and we got to talking about a certain teacher. I couldn't come up with the woman's name, and neither could Joy, even though we both knew the person we had in mind. We kept talking about "What's-her-name."

Joy glanced over at David just then, who was sitting in his wheelchair and listening to the conversation. His eyes were absolutely dancing. It dawned on both of us—*he knew the name we couldn't recall!* Everything within him wanted to fill in the blank. He was dying to talk, but he just couldn't articulate the words. He couldn't find a pathway to let us know. He was frustrated, and so were we.

But we were encouraged at the same time to discover how much he remembered from the past. Somehow we would find a way to release him from his prison.

In Search of Another Chance

The summer morning in June was already getting hot as we loaded up to head for the Spokane evaluation. It would be as long a trip as the one from Lewiston in November—only this time we had no access to a well-equipped ambulance. We were on our own, spreading out a mattress in the back of our old Jeep, where David would have to lie for hours. His wheelchair was strapped to the roof rack.

Once again, travel gave me time to reflect. What if this trip turned out to be pointless? What if Dr. Moise said the same thing as Dr. Smith had: that David was a hopeless case and further therapy would just be a waste? *Oh, Lord,* I silently prayed, *please make a way for us. Just a crack in the door. You love David as much as we do. Please help us get him the attention he needs.*

When we rolled up to the entrance of Sacred Heart Hospital, we were quite a sight, tugging David off the Jeep tailgate and getting him into his wheelchair. After so many hours of riding, he was stiffer than ever. But once we got him into the examining room, the day took on a brighter hue. Dr. Moise turned out to be a gracious and caring woman. She had read David's file in advance, and she showed interest in what we were trying to do for our son.

She began asking him to do very simple things, such as blinking his eyes and sticking out his tongue. She got him to raise his left arm, then his right. David seemed to be aware that this was an important moment and he should do his best.

I could tell she was doing more than just giving individual commands—she was sizing up the whole person, watching David closely and taking notice of the look in his eyes. She spent a total of forty-five minutes conducting her assessment.

When it was over, we got no immediate indication of her conclusions. We drove home wondering what her report would say. When eventually I saw a copy in Dr. Bracchi's office, however, I could not help appreciating the tone of the opening sentence: "Thank you for sending this interesting patient to me." She didn't view David as a problem or even a tragedy; instead, she found him *interesting*. In the end, she expressed her professional opinion that further therapy would indeed benefit this young man.

My heart leaped with joy at that news. Her report was quickly forwarded to the Medicaid office in Olympia, the state capital, along with other documentation. The wheels began to turn, and on Monday, July 2, 1990, we were welcomed at Good Samaritan Hospital in Puyallup for the beginning of a whole new chapter in David's recovery.

The impressive brick building sat on the side of a very steep hill. The minute we walked into the therapy center, we gasped at the size. Unlike the small departments we had seen before, this facility was nearly the size of a school gymnasium. It had five mat tables, an array of exercise bicycles, several sets of parallel bars—everything one could ask for. I looked around and thought, *What a turning point for David. And to think it all started with Cara Anderson.* My heart felt a fresh rush of gratitude for her intervention with Dr. Bracchi that night.

The therapy pool likewise was absolutely huge compared to what I had seen in other facilities. Every staff member we met seemed to exude competence. And again, as in Lewiston, family housing was available just across the street.

We were immediately impressed with the warmth and compassion of Dr. Sherburne Heath, founder and director of the rehabilitation unit. A gentle man with gray hair who was nearing retirement, he said hello and got David headed toward his assigned room. Then he invited us into his office. "Tell me about David," he asked with genuine interest. "What was he like before the accident? Tell me about his accomplishments."

Of course I had no trouble responding to that kind of inquiry. I described how active David had been, what a good student he was, and how much he loved life and his Lord. This opened the way for Dr. Heath to reveal his own faith and say, "I really believe that God is the ultimate healer. We just try to assist him here."

He wanted to know as many details about the accident as we could provide. He took notes as we talked. I was impressed with his thorough regard for the complete patient.

The regimen of therapy sessions began the very next morning, with various people working on everything from stretching to balance—and even trying to get David to speak. I watched intently and took notes. Often I shot video as well so I'd have something to review in depth when we got home.

Every Tuesday the staff held a team conference to document how far they were getting with David. The physical therapist would report, then the occupational therapist, the neuropsychologist, the speech therapist, the recreational specialist, and others. These excerpts from the written summaries make for fascinating reading:

JULY 10, 1990
His performance and cooperation are enhanced with rewards: candy or fruit juice. At other times cooperation improves with

repeated instruction. . . . Patient requires maximal assistance to stand in the parallel bars. On mats he requires moderate to maximal assistance to roll. . . . He is now propelling his wheelchair minimally, tends to veer to the side. . . .

In self-care areas he is able to put on a shirt, although he responds poorly to instruction. It is felt that he should be able to do more in this area and this will be pursued.

JULY 17, 1990

Physical therapist has him scheduled into the pool today for the first time. . . . Overall, he is more alert and variably cooperative with treatment. . . . He is noted to have nearly pulled himself up to standing in the parallel bars.

. . . An alphabet board and pictures have been tried as a means of communication. He does not point accurately to either pictures or letters. He needs cues for virtually every activity. David still has no speech or phonation.

JULY 24, 1990

David . . . has shown more gains the past week than previously . . . more emotional responses, that is, facial expression, attempts to smile, and greater awareness of environment in contrast to his very flat affect on admission.

. . . He has been able to stack 31 cones with his left hand against a five-pound weight; he stacks 20 cones on the right against a three-pound weight.

. . . His nurse notes that he is still incontinent of urine. His bowel program is being switched to an evening program. The patient's mother is concerned about weight gain, has asked to have his diet cut down. [That's for sure; he was ballooning up past 200 pounds! I knew I'd be back to lifting him myself once we got home, so I urged them to control the calories, please.]

And so it continued. By the end of July he was navigating two lengths of the parallel bars, with major assistance, of course. We got him out to a baseball game, where he paid attention at least some of the time. By early August he could propel his wheelchair one hundred feet, although he had trouble setting the brake, which was on his right (weaker) side. He could actually play the card game Uno, which was great for helping him sort colors and numbers.

The hospital doors had a security system with an alarm that would ring if a patient attempted to leave without permission. One day when I wasn't around, David wheeled himself toward the exit, knowing that the vending machines were not far ahead. Naturally he didn't have any money in his pocket, so it would have done him no good to get there. But he still wanted to look at the treats. The bell went off, and he sheepishly had to retreat.

On a different day, I took him outside for a ride in the warm summer sun. The only problem was that I had neglected to affix his seat belt, and when we started down the steep sidewalk in front of the hospital, the weight was more than I could restrain. I began struggling to hang on against the downward momentum.

Soon David was sliding out of his seat! I panicked. I dug in my heels to keep the wheelchair from completely running away on its own. But there was no way I could reach forward to pull him back from scooting down the hill while struggling with his chair.

At that terrible moment two people in a dental office across the street saw my predicament and came running to rescue us. I thanked them profusely. Then I turned around and headed back up to the hospital. No more adventuring for me.

"I'm so sorry, I almost lost control on the hill," I confessed when I got back to the nurses' station. "It's all my fault—I didn't buckle him in before we left. I didn't realize it was so steep!"

They forgave me, checking David over for injuries. He had only one small bruise on his bottom from hitting the footrest. Otherwise, he would be all right, despite his mother's negligence.

A Cup Half Full

As I watched the various specialists do their best to get David moving and relating, I could not stop thanking them. What I loved most about Dr. Heath was his way of always focusing on what David *could* do, rather than on what he couldn't do. For him, the cup was always half full, not half empty. "You know, Leone," he said to me one day, "I just think there's more going on in there than he ever lets me know. He's a fine young man."

I don't mean to imply that they thought normality was just around the corner. The Good Samaritan staff was realistic. They openly stated that David would never speak. They saw no reason to expect he would ever control his body eliminations on his own. But his ability to get at least some food into his mouth was improving, as was self-dressing and physical endurance.

"I don't see any reason why you can't care for him at home," Dr. Heath concluded, knowing that Medicaid funding wouldn't sustain him at the hospital forever. "We will help you figure out what you need, and we'll be glad to have you bring him back again from time to time for reassessment. We want you to be able to take care of David the way you want to do it."

When we finally checked out of Good Samaritan on August 24, we had learned so much. We were no longer ama-

Bill and David join me for a tender moment just before Steve's birth.

My five precious sons in October 1983 (clockwise from center): Bud, Rob, David, Bill, and Steve.

David was a talented high school athlete. He played football until he tore a muscle; after that, he took up wrestling.

David goofs off in the kitchen with friends in 1987. He was fun loving and enjoyed playing pranks on people.

David and his infamous Triumph Spitfire. It broke down often, making his motorcycle a necessary backup.

David's brain was severely injured in a motorcycle accident on October 15, 1989. This image was captured from a video taken after his surgery five days later. I spent many hours praying and keeping watch over him when the doctors weren't sure he would even survive.

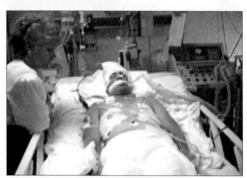

We call the photo at right "Love's Hall of Fame." It shows 24 friends who volunteered in teams for an unproven rehabilitation method called patterning (shown above). These friends were a crucial part of David's recovery.

After long and arduous rehabilitation, we were thrilled when David relearned to crawl at home.

Here I am in our "budget rehab" center (our garage), helping David's muscles regain their strength and relearn how to operate.

With God's Word inspiring him, David works hard in the garage. The whole family helped with his workouts.

BUT THEY THAT WAIT UPON THE LORD SHALL RENEW THEIR STRENGTH THEY SHALL MOUNT UP WINGS AS EAGLES; THEY SHALL RUN AND NOT BE WEARY AND THEY SHALL WALK AND NOT FAINT ISAIAH 40:31

My son Bill assists David as he attempts to navigate the sidewalk.

My husband, Dale, with David, Steve, and me. Dale has been a loving, dedicated father and stepfather; I never could have succeeded without him.

Two women who made a huge difference: Linda Sharp (left) stopped at the accident and prayed, holding David's hand until the ambulance arrived. Cara Anderson, RN, (right) spoke up for further rehab when David was about to be sent to a nursing home.

Photo of Bill, David, and me before a cousin's wedding

In 1993, the new David greets his niece, Caitlin McRae, with his trademark gesture of delight. He's not the same man he was before the accident, but his life is precious to us and to God.

teurs. We determined to go back to Yakima and get busy duplicating as many of their tactics as possible.

Our two vehicles would have to sit in the driveway, we decided, as the garage became our center for what we called "budget rehab." Dale began calling on some of his construction buddies to help; a carpenter built us a seven-foot-square mat table, for example. At the fabric shop I bought boat vinyl and two-inch foam, then took it to an upholsterer. He assembled the mat for just thirty-five dollars, and that even included zippers.

Meanwhile, a sheet metal company made a set of parallel bars plus a standing table, which is a tall frame with straps to hold a person vertical while he or she does various tasks on a chest-high fiberglass tray, such as getting pegs into a Peg-Board.

The list of items kept growing until it included:

- cheap plastic glasses for stacking
- arm weights
- puzzles
- paper, pencils, marking pens
- alphabet cards
- a blackboard
- beanbags for tossing into a basket
- simple math flash cards
- rubber alphabet letters
- a large balancing ball for improving balance
- a round bolster cushion for stomach stretches
- plastic blow tubes to build diaphragm strength
- a large calendar

- a clock
- two kerosene heaters and an electric heater to keep us going when winter arrived

Total outlay of money: around $2,000. To purchase all this through a medical supply company would have cost three to four times as much.

On a large schedule pad I wrote out our regimen. Each day had its slot for physical therapy, occupational therapy, and speech therapy, just as I had seen these things done in Puyallup. I knew that high structure was good for someone with a head injury.

But the most important words I posted were those across the inside of the garage door. They were printed on a huge computer-generated banner displaying our theme Scripture for this effort. The verse from Isaiah 40:31 (KJV) set the tone for what we aspired to do: "They that wait upon the LORD shall renew their strength; they shall mount up with wings as eagles; they shall run, and not be weary; and they shall walk, and not faint." With the Lord's help, this would be our goal.

SEVEN

A-B-C-D-E-F-G

By now, the attitude of "can do," or at least "let's try,"
was so entrenched in me that I began pushing to
achieve things others said were impossible. David
would never speak—oh, really? Well, it wouldn't
hurt to see what could be done. If we failed, it
would only mean he was left in the same condition.
But if we succeeded . . .

All this was based on the premise that the human
brain is more than just a machine. It is not like, say, a
car, where if the transmission is broken, there's nothing the pistons or the radiator can do about it—each
part has its own function, and that's that. The brain,
by contrast, has billions of living cells. And there's at
least some evidence that these cells can reorient
themselves, picking up new capabilities to compensate for other cells that are damaged or even missing.

In other words, *persistent vegetative state* doesn't have to mean *permanent* vegetative state.

Yes, David had lost five centimeters of his left temporal lobe, the speech center of the brain. But perhaps other parts of the brain would rise to the challenge. I had noticed that whenever I rolled him over, he let out a groan. I assumed this was due to scar tissue from the insertion of the chest tubes in the winter. But the pattern was consistent: Every rollover produced a groan.

"David, let's work on this," I said one morning. "The doctors don't think you're ever going to be able to talk. But I just think the Lord's got something better for you. If you can groan when I roll you over, maybe you can start putting those sounds into words."

Time and time again, I would roll him over and say, "Hear that, David? You're making a sound. You're using your vocal cords. Let's do it again." We did this hundreds of times.

Much later, I read somewhere that talking requires the use of some two hundred muscles; it's not a small feat. We take it for granted. But with David, I was trying to marshal all these muscles to put out a sound, any kind of sound.

I have videotapes that are downright silly of me leaning over him on the daybed asking him to imitate me: "Get me up! Get me up! Get me up! Say it, David. You want to get up this morning, right? Okay, ask me. Get me up!" His grunts were not even close to being intelligible, but at least he was attempting to repeat what I was chanting in his face.

I found that if I pushed on his diaphragm while he was lying down, I could get a stronger sound. I would push rhythmically as I urged him to say a simple phrase, and he began to make the association: *If I push from my stomach area, I can make a noise in my throat.* This worked much better when he was lying down than when he was sitting up; when he was vertical, the volume level dropped to a whisper.

The day we had been dreaming of finally came in October—actual intelligible words out of his mouth. I was doing my typical coaxing: "David, say this: Candy bar! Candy bar! Candy bar!" playing to his sweet tooth, of course.

And then, in a high-pitched voice, the reply came back: "Candy bar!"

"Way to go, David!" I screamed. I hugged him so hard I almost tipped the wheelchair over. He smiled his biggest smile as well. He knew he had pleased his mama.

Hard at Work

All this was in addition to the conventional therapy work in the garage. We stretched and rolled and stood up in the parallel bars. We stacked cones as we had learned in Puyallup. We did discrimination drills, in which I would place four objects in front of him and say, "Okay, here is a ball, a bird feather, a bell, and a pencil. Pick up the bell."

To do so required not only thinking through the concepts but also visually recognizing the items—and we found that David's eyesight was not 100 percent. The head injury and subsequent surgery had robbed him of some peripheral vision on the right side, so that he actually did not see objects beyond about the midline of his right eye's field of view. We began trying to stretch that boundary, holding up a large card with black-and-white stripes (called a zebra card) and moving it toward the right as he tracked along.

All this was my full-time job. I hardly stopped to realize that I was working at this rehabilitation nearly 24-7. Dale was putting in tons of time as well, even though he had a business to try to rescue from the rocks. One time he was reviewing simple math flash cards with David. "What's this one?" he asked, holding up 4 + 1. David held up five fingers. Next came 3 + 4. David responded with seven fingers.

"Good," Dale said. "Now how about 5 + 3?" he asked, holding up another card.

David raised just two fingers.

"No, that's not right. What's 5 + 3? Come on, Dave, you can get this."

Again, just two fingers.

"David, you're not thinking," Dale scolded, turning around the card. And to his embarrassment, he found he had misread the sign. The card actually said "5 − 3"!

Bill remembers not being able to hang out with his friends after high school. When they'd say, "Hey, let's go get a Coke" or "Let's play some soccer," he would reply, "Nah, I need to get home to help with my brother."

Dr. Bracchi, though privately skeptical that we could manage David at home (as he later confessed), was affirming whenever he spoke to us. His chart notes reveal the following:

OCTOBER 16, 1990
[one year plus a day after the accident]
Incredible progress. I am basically thrilled.

NOVEMBER 27, 1990
Doing incredibly well.

By the end of October, David's language skills were rapidly expanding. He could say the months of the year and the letters of the alphabet, provided I kept pushing on his diaphragm. He could count to one hundred. He could use scissors to cut out a paper circle. When we put his old instrument, a trombone, up to his lips, he could blow a somewhat airy note.

By November we had him buttoning his shirt. We were making real headway—in large part because I kept pushing. I suppose I enjoyed a special authority none of the other nurses and therapists had: I was his mother. He had been conditioned to obey me for twenty-one years. Whenever I said, "Okay, David, let's get to work," he just assumed he had to comply.

But not always. Occasionally he would balk. He wouldn't get onto the mat, or he wouldn't do the discrimination drill. One effect of a head injury such as his is that it robs a person of initiative and willpower. I was basically the replacement now; I provided his will. And every so often, he didn't appreciate my pushing him.

One week he got into a streak of locking up on me. By Friday I was genuinely mad at him. "David, if you're going to act like a two-year-old, I'm going to treat you like a two-year-old!" I said. I got my flyswatter and gave him five swats on the bottom—which was well padded with his diaper, of course. So it certainly didn't inflict any actual pain. But the activity brought back a memory to his mind that he needed to do what Mom said.

Even then, I was apprehensive for a moment. *Oh, boy, I can see the headlines now,* I thought, *"Mother Beats Brain-Injured Son."* It turned out to be the only time I resorted to corporal discipline.

Most of the time I could get my way with rewards. That was my main strategy in tackling the next huge mountain the experts had said we'd never fully conquer: bathroom control. I'd been told he would be in diapers for the rest of his life. But since I was the main person changing the diapers now, I decided I'd like to challenge that prediction.

One day I parked David in his wheelchair about six feet from the kitchen counter, put a Butterfinger candy bar on the counter, and handed him a plastic urinal. "Guess what, David," I announced. "As soon as you go in this urinal, you can have the candy bar!"

He stared at me blankly, then quickly returned to focus on the candy bar. His face lit up. Oh, how he wanted it! "Use the urinal first, and it's yours," I reinforced.

I'm sure this kind of bribery would never pass regulations in the therapy profession. But we moms can get away with almost anything.

Fifteen minutes later, I had the results I wanted.

I held up the urinal and cried, "David, this is liquid gold! You can do this! I knew you could!" He began reaching for the candy bar, and I started breaking off little chunks for him to enjoy.

From that moment on, I kept handing him the urinal every couple of hours, and he quickly managed to stay dry throughout the daytime hours. It was a wonderful step of progress. He began sensing the physical urge to go, and he would point to himself if necessary.

But what about nighttime? Could I ever get him beyond the diaper stage for all those hours? I knew that if achieving daytime continence had been like climbing Mount Rainier, this would be Everest.

"We're not going to use a diaper tonight," I announced to David one evening a few months later as I got him ready for his small bed in the downstairs den. "I'll sleep right here beside you on the floor. I'll wake you up every hour to see if you have to go."

We made it through that first night without incident. This became my routine. Eventually I observed that I could get away with two-hour instead of one-hour intervals. This gave me a little more rest.

Though there were a few wet nights here and there, he was mostly continent throughout this period. Finally, however, came the night I will never forget. I awakened him around three in the morning and asked if he needed to go. "No," came the reply.

About half an hour later, I awoke for some reason and decided to check on him, just to be sure.

He was wet.

I lost it. "David, I asked you just thirty minutes ago if you had to go, and you said you didn't! This is ridiculous. Now you're all wet, and the bed's all wet. What good does it do for me to be up all hours of the night asking you if you don't tell me the truth? I can't believe this!"

I took a deep breath and then continued my tirade. "I'll tell you what—this time, you're going to clean yourself up. Sit up and start taking off your T-shirt. I'm not going to do it for you. You're going to have to take care of the problem *you* caused."

He began to struggle with his wet shirt. In his condition, he tugged and pulled pathetically, making only tiny progress. I felt so sorry for him, even in my anger. I sat in the corner and bawled. I yearned to help him, but I knew he had to learn not to expect pampering for the rest of his life. The whole ordeal of changing his shirt and shorts took more than an hour.

I wasn't cruel enough to make him change the sheets too; I took care of that for him. Finally, we settled down to sleep again. "David," I said before turning out the light, "the lesson here is that you've got to do your part. You can't assume that I'll just take care of everything." He nodded.

That was pretty much the last wet night we had. Soon we got to the place where I could trust him so much that I'd just hang a couple of urinals on the bedpost and go upstairs to sleep; he would take care of his own needs throughout the night. I'd come back the next morning and congratulate him enthusiastically on being so responsible.

Then came the night when I forgot to place the urinals within reach. I just totally spaced out for some reason. The next morning when I came into his room, it suddenly dawned on me what I'd done—but there was David, already awake, dry, and grinning from ear to ear. Why? He had waited all night, then finally pulled a large cream-colored ceramic bell from the end table and used it shortly after dawn as a substitute! He held up the bell like it was a trophy.

"David, you're amazing!" I cried. "You thought up a solution, didn't you?" He giggled. "Well, I've learned one thing for sure—you definitely have problem-solving skills! So don't try pulling the wool over my eyes. You're smart!"

Family Team

While all this had been going on, the rest of the family was working right alongside me, sharing the joys and the sorrows alike. Rob, my second son, returned from the navy in early

October 1990. He'd had very little access to communication during the past year because whenever his nuclear submarine went underwater, messages could not get through.

One time back during the Lewiston days, his sub had surfaced for radio traffic. Rob had been able to get a thirty-word update that David was still alive and stabilizing. But most of the time he was left wondering.

When he finally arrived at our home that fall, a year after the accident, I could tell he was shaken by what he saw. He would hold up photos—even photos of himself—and David would be clueless as to what they were. "Mom, I guess I just thought he'd be better by now," Rob confessed to me in private. "He's messed up forever, isn't he? I had to walk away just now so he wouldn't see me crying."

"I know, Son," I replied. "It's not the kind of situation anybody can just fix with a military order, is it? We're in this for the long haul."

Bud and his wife, Lori, came to Dale and me early on and said, "You guys need a break once in a while. You can't keep doing this seven days a week. We'd like to take David over to our place for a four-day stretch—say, Thursday through Sunday—once a month, so you can rest and catch your breath." What sweethearts they were.

Bud even traded in their car for a pickup truck so he could haul all the necessary gear to their apartment in the rough part of town. One day Bud was pulling David up the front steps in his wheelchair when a wheel got caught in the railing. He couldn't lift any farther, he couldn't let go, and he couldn't get the apparatus free. David, he could tell, was petrified.

"Hey, Mario!" he yelled at the top of his lungs to his

cocaine-dealing, hard-drinking neighbor. "Come help me! Help!"

Fortunately the man was relatively sober at that moment and helped Bud out of his predicament.

On another evening, Bud and Lori ventured to take David to his first movie since the accident. Bud asked to borrow our Jeep, since all three of them would be riding together. By now, unlike the earlier trip to Spokane in this vehicle, David could sit up in the passenger seat.

What Bud didn't know was that sometimes the right front door would freeze up and refuse to open. They got to the theater parking lot, and suddenly there was no convenient way to get David out. Bud tugged and tugged, but the door wouldn't release.

"What could we do but drag him out through the driver-side door?" he said when he told me the story. "Lori took his feet first, and I caught his upper torso—it looked for all the world like we were dragging a dead body out of the Jeep! I wonder what onlookers must have thought."

But eventually they made it inside the theater. Bud bought his brother a bag of M&M's. Every so often during the movie, David's hold on the bag would relax so that a few candies would fall out, going *plink-plink-plink* down the slanted floor of the theater.

This adventure was nothing, however, compared to the time in mid-December when they took David to a young-marrieds Christmas party. Some twenty couples were there, and of course they knew David and welcomed him warmly. The lights were twinkling as carols played and people stood around sipping hot cider and talking, enjoying the holiday atmosphere.

Then all of a sudden, a stench began to fill the room. David had messed his pants in a big way. There was no ignoring the odor; it was too strong. People looked at each other awkwardly, trying to figure out what to say or do. The whole party came to a crashing halt.

"Uh, well, folks, I think we'll be leaving now," Bud announced with a red face. He and Lori made their exit, pushing David's wheelchair out the door as quickly as they could. People tried to think of gracious things to say as they headed toward home to start the cleanup process.

Bud told me later that of all the deeds of service he performed for his brother in those days, wiping him was the hardest. "You're a mom; you got used to this when we were all little," he said. "But for a brother . . . it's different." He added, however, that one of the first times he got a direct response was the day he was wiping David too forcefully, and he began to complain, "Ow! Ow! Ow!" At least they were communicating, man to man.

We were taking life one event at a time, doing what we could to bring David back from the fog. The newspapers were filled that Christmas season with stories about Nancy Cruzan, the young Missouri woman who had been left in a persistent vegetative state after a car accident seven years before. In that situation, her family wanted to pull her feeding tube. The first court agreed with their wishes, but the Missouri Supreme Court said no, and the case went all the way to the U.S. Supreme Court. There it was decided that Missouri could keep blocking the removal unless there was "clear and convincing evidence" of Nancy's intentions from when she was still conscious. The family finally came up with three witnesses to bolster their position, and the feeding tube came out. She died the day after Christmas at the age of thirty-three.

I did not presume to question or judge the Cruzan family's position; I had not walked in their shoes or been forced to weigh the medical factors they faced. The story did make me think, however, about the hard choices people face on the edge of death and life. I gave thanks that season that our David was showing signs of progress and that our family was united in pressing ahead for more of them.

Ups and Downs

By January David was playing simple video games on the television screen, guiding a car along a racetrack with a joystick. He'd crash his car often, which only brought a big smile to his face.

He was better at playing games such as Connect Four, which contains a vertical tray into which a player and an opponent drop red and black checkers, back and forth; the first person to place four in a row wins. Cheryl Strauss, our next-door neighbor, came over to play this often with David, who frequently beat her.

Other neighbors were less friendly. One of them called the police to do something about the fact that David's red Triumph was still sitting out at the curb. As mentioned before, we had no garage space for vehicles; every square foot was consumed with rehab equipment.

Sure enough, a ticket showed up on the windshield of the sports car one day.

I was ticked off. I called the police department and asked to speak with the officer who had written the citation.

"Who in the world had the nerve to complain about this?" I demanded. "Don't they know our son is terribly head injured and we've turned the whole garage into a therapy room? *None* of our cars will fit inside now, even though it's wintertime. For heaven's sake."

"I don't know the person's name," he calmly replied, "but I'll tell you what: You just go ahead and leave that car on the street—and if the ticket comes up as delinquent, I'll throw it in the trash. I understand what you're going through. Don't worry about it."

On February 9—David's twenty-third birthday—Bud and Lori threw a big party for him. Some thirty people showed up, and it was a wonderful occasion. (No quick exits this time.) As I looked over the crowd, I noticed that few of David's high school friends had come, however. Dwayne Taylor, a wonderful young man, was there, but he seemed to be the only one. We had heard that another fellow David had played football with had found his first visit with David too much to handle. He told mutual friends around town, "You don't want to go see David. It's too hard."

Well, it *was* hard; there was no denying that. Even Bill, now a junior in high school, struggled with the tragedy we were working to overcome. I could tell by his silence at times that Bill was troubled. Why couldn't God have kept all this from happening in the first place? he wondered. At times Bill's vexation showed in crankiness toward me or staying out late at night. I worried about him and urged him to see Pastor Wayne and talk about what he was feeling, which was of some help.

One time when Pastor Wayne could sense that the whole family was struggling, he took an unusual step in a Sunday morning service. "We've been praying for David McRae and the Nunley family," he said, "and I appreciate all the ways many of you have been helping out. But today, I'd like us to take a few minutes to offer special words of encouragement.

"You'll notice that we've placed a microphone on a stand at the head of each aisle. Think back to a time in your life when God has picked you up and sustained you through difficulty by means of a Scripture verse. Find that verse in your Bible, please, and then come to one of the mikes and share it."

Soon there were long lines of people on both sides of the church, waiting their turn to speak. One after another told how God had strengthened them when they were down and read the relevant Scriptures. Some of them even dated their experience, such as, "Back in 1986 when I was diagnosed with cancer . . ." It was a powerful time that lasted fifteen or twenty minutes. We sat there and simply listened, soaking in the uplifting Word of God.

I also gradually learned that it would be all right for me to *ask* for help when I needed it. In February 1991, Dale was going to have to return to Hawaii for another stint of work before he could finish that chapter of his life for good. I swallowed my pride and called COPES, the local office of respite care. "Would it ever be possible to have someone come help me with the heavier physical therapy workouts we're trying to provide for our son?" I asked. I went on to explain the circumstances.

"Yes, we think that can be arranged," the man said. Soon Ron Jackson began showing up five days a week for ninety minutes each morning, putting David through his paces in the garage. Ron was muscular as well as likable, and he demanded sit-ups and pull-ups without mercy. He got David out on the sidewalk using his frame walker, pushing him to his limits. We bought an air-resistance exercise bike with high dual-action handlebars for Ron to use, something I couldn't have managed on my own.

To this day, whenever we show David a picture of Ron Jackson, he grimaces and says, "Bad! Bad!" We laugh and say, "Oh, no, David, he did you a lot of good!" We ended up giving Ron the red Triumph in appreciation for all he did.

Another form of outside assistance came in response to my appeal to the state for support from David's father. I wrote to the Office of Support Enforcement explaining that Leo had not paid child support for any of the four boys for more than a decade and that David's present condition certainly warranted it. They contacted him in Alaska and managed to get a flow of five hundred dollars a month started, which helped cover our many expenses. This continued for three years before fading away.

Further contact, however, was almost more trouble than it was worth. Leo showed up in town unannounced one Thursday, leading into a weekend when David was at Bud and Lori's. He asked if he could see David.

"Sure," Bud replied. "How about dinner tomorrow night at six o'clock?"

"Good. See you then."

But in fact, he didn't show up until eight-thirty. By then, my spunky daughter-in-law had put the food away.

"Sorry, Dad," Bud said at the door. "David needs to get to sleep now. How about coming back tomorrow morning? Nine o'clock would be good."

It was agreed.

Bud set his alarm for five-thirty the next morning to be sure he had time to get David up, sponge-bathed, fed, and dressed for his visitor. "Dad's coming over to see you!" he cheerfully announced.

The hours passed, one after another. The doorbell never rang. Another disappointment in a long line of broken dreams. Bud didn't know what to say to David. Both of them stared into space, wondering.

Word eventually got back to us that Leo had been out drinking Friday night. He couldn't make it up for a nine o'clock commitment the next morning. He returned to Alaska without further contacting any of us.

Bud has a pretty gentle personality, but in this case, he could not suppress a touch of sarcasm. Three months later he sent a postcard to his father that read, "Um, since you haven't yet arrived, I assume you're not coming over to see David after all."

Back to Puyallup

In late March we headed back to Good Samaritan Hospital in Puyallup for a reassessment. It was such a joy to see Dr. Heath and the staff again during our two-week stay. They saw what David had learned since the previous summer and applauded his progress.

He spent a great deal of time in the pool, which was warmer than our local YMCA pool and therefore more agreeable to David. The therapists also worked on getting him to sit up from a prone position by himself, pushing on the palms of his hands. They coached him on improving his gait while walking in the parallel bars. As for me, I gained valuable instruction on where to go next.

The *Yakima Herald-Republic* ran a front-page feature on Sunday, June 23, 1991, about our work with David. Pictures showed our hard work in the garage but also the fun of playing a game together as a family. The article described the accident and all the subsequent efforts, both by medical professionals and untrained friends, to try to reclaim what had been lost.

"Last week, McRae hoisted himself out of his wheelchair without help," it read. "He combed his hair, won at Bingo, and counted past 100. His vocabulary has topped 125 words. . . . Other times he sorts papers, or drives a golf cart, or solves puzzles."[3]

We were glad to showcase the progress of the past months. We hoped it would encourage other families who were facing similar trauma. In fact, the article spread out to a larger circle than we expected, as newspapers in Wenatchee, Pullman, Spokane, and elsewhere picked it up for their editions.

Through the article, we were able to give credit where credit was due: to our Lord's sustaining hand. "If we could have chosen our path, we probably wouldn't have chosen this one," I told the reporter. "We do know that we'll never have the old David back. But the Lord has given us a new David, and that's the one we encourage and support."

EIGHT

The Foundation Is Missing

Parents who are trying to cope with head-injured children naturally gravitate toward each other. When we run into one another in the hospital, at a doctor's office, or at rehab, we encourage each other not to give up. We share any pieces of promising information we've found.

"Have you ever heard about patterning?" a woman named Anne Massong said to me one day in 1991. Her son, Robert, had been as gravely damaged as David had.

"No—what's that?" I replied.

"Well, I don't know very much about it, but they say it's a therapy you can do at home that helps rehabilitate the brain. There's a family named Graham down in northern California who's using it, and they say it's helping a lot."

Soon I was in touch with Don and Meredith Graham, whose twenty-year-old daughter, Melissa, had been knocked off her bicycle by a pickup truck that crossed the yellow line. Her condition sounded all too familiar: a deep coma in the beginning weeks, then gradual flickers of awareness, but still profound loss of function. Doctors had predicted she wouldn't last a year due to lung or urinary tract infections that were almost sure to overwhelm her.

But now, four years later, the Grahams were busy rebuilding Melissa's capabilities. Their strategy was patterning, a technique developed in the 1950s on the East Coast, at what was then called the Rehabilitation Center at Philadelphia. An enterprising physical therapist named Glenn Doman and his colleagues had theorized that the brain could relearn its functions the same way it had learned them the first time in early childhood. How does a baby learn to walk? It doesn't suddenly stand up one day and start putting one foot in front of the other. Instead, the baby first learns to crawl.

What if a brain-injured person were put on a large table, Doman said, and then surrounded with five aides (one for each arm and each leg, plus the head) who proceeded to mimic the crawling motion? Would the activity in essence travel "backward" through the central nervous system to inform the brain that this is how crawling is done? Would these routines become embedded enough that the brain cells could direct the body to reproduce the actions later on? Doman and his colleagues began experimenting, and the results were impressive.

Once a person can crawl, the foundation is laid for pulling himself up onto furniture (as every parent knows). From that point, the next step is to stand upright—and then to walk.

The Grahams sent us Glenn Doman's book *What to Do about Your Brain-Injured Child*.[4] I also devoured a dramatic seven-page photo feature that had run in *Look* magazine way back in the early sixties, which told more than 7 million readers how a nine-year-old boy who had been hit by a car was being restored by this therapy at the Philadelphia clinic. His first name, ironically, was also David. The story said:

> David's treatment is based on artificially imposing on the damaged brain the patterns of movement (crawling, creeping, etc.) that the brain cannot reproduce itself. Associated with these damaged areas, or levels, are speech, vision, manual dexterity. . . . In a matter of weeks, an undamaged part of David's brain got the message, took over the work of the damaged part and made it possible for him to move his arms and legs. . . .
>
> The germ of this revolutionary form of therapy was conceived many years ago by Dr. Temple Fay of Philadelphia. . . . Greater success has been realized by this method than by any other in that it treats the injured area, the brain, and not the symptoms of the injury, spastic limbs and slurred speech. It does not use braces or wheelchairs or other traditionally employed devices. It works on the assumption that, when some of the brain cells are damaged, all is not lost—since there are roughly 30 billion cells, and all of them educable.[5]

In the midseventies a registered nurse from the Philadelphia team had come out to the Northwest to head up a branch clinic in Woodburn, Oregon, about thirty miles south of Portland. Her name was Florence Scott. The Grahams urged me to get in touch with her.

I was on the phone immediately. We set an appointment for June 25, 1991, at 9:45 a.m. David would receive a half-day evaluation, culminating in recommendations for treatment we could do at home. I fired off a videotape of daily life with David so Florence could see in advance what we were up against.

When we rolled up to the Woodburn clinic that summer day, it became clear that we were outside the boundaries of traditional medicine. A handmade sign, "Northwest Neurodevelopmental Training Center," marked the humble building, and I noticed a thrift shop in the back that was apparently needed to help keep the doors open. Dr. Bracchi had already advised me that patterning got no endorsements in medical literature; no MDs were saying it was effective over the long term. Even our good friend Dr. Heath in Puyallup had said he had heard of it, but "all it really does is just wear out the families who try to do it," he concluded. Obviously, no insurance program was going to pick up the tab for this.

Even though I admired both physicians greatly, I wasn't going to let their reluctance keep me from exploring this alternative. After all, I was the one with daily care of a head-injured son who, if put onto the floor, could not move an inch. He could shuffle his feet if we stood him up in the parallel bars or in a frame walker, but beyond that, he was frozen in space, despite all our hard work. Could patterning change that, even to a modest degree?

"Welcome," Florence Scott said that morning. She was a short middle-aged woman with dark hair and glasses. "I enjoyed watching your video, and now I get to meet David in person!"

For the next several hours she tested David on a number of different functions. She was very thorough and very kind. Eventually she said to me, "I can really appreciate the effort you and the rest of the family have been putting into this young man. I know you've been doing a great deal, and I applaud you for that. But the truth is, you've been trying to put on the roof before the foundation is in. We need to go back to the beginning and take developmental steps in their natural sequence.

"Have you thought about the fact that babies never learn to crawl or walk while they're on their back? Only when you put them on their tummy do they start becoming mobile, getting off that blanket. But what happens to every brain-injured person in an institution? They lie there flat on their back, day after day. No wonder they never get moving.

"Your whole route to making headway with David is to work with him on his stomach."

She brought out charts that showed how patterning works, step by step. "You'll need a padded table at least thirty-two inches off the floor," she said. "Then you'll need five people at a time. As you work with David, you will take care to keep his spine straight; you're not twisting him into some kind of pretzel here. You simply and carefully turn his head to the left as a team member pulls his left arm upward, so his hand is close to his face, and simultaneously another team member bends his left leg, with ninety-degree angles at both the hip and the knee. Meanwhile, the right arm and leg stay straight down.

"Then you do the reverse: You turn the head to the right

and bring the right arm and leg upward, while returning the left arm and leg back to a resting position, pointing down. Back and forth, back and forth, you keep going for a full five minutes. By then David will be tired, and so will all of you! So you rest for twenty minutes or so, then go at it again."

Soon the clinic's staff members had David up on a table demonstrating all this, while I watched in amazement. I could tell David hardly knew what to think. He didn't resist, but he was so chronically stiff that they really had to push and tug to achieve what they wanted.

"Four repetitions of all this make up a daily workout," she explained as the patterning continued. "You have to be committed to this every day in order to achieve the results." She described two alternate rhythms as well: one done while the patient lies on his back, the other a cross-pattern that turns the head in the opposite direction of what the limbs are doing. All of this was reinforced with materials that bore the newer name of the Philadelphia center, the Institutes for the Achievement of Human Potential.[6] The main idea, I was beginning to grasp, was that instead of the brain telling the extremities what to do, the extremities instruct the brain over and over, *Here's what we're doing. Good idea, don't you think?* And eventually, the brain agrees.

This was a watershed day for David and our family. At the end of the session, I gathered up the resource materials, paid the fee, and said to Florence Scott, "Thank you so much for giving us hope. We are definitely going to go back to Yakima and try this!"

We loaded David back into the Jeep and started up the interstate. Inside, I was brimming with excitement. But I was also overwhelmed with the thought of changing our whole approach. Should we really drop so many of the things we'd been doing? I was also fearful as I thought about the practicalities. How in the world would I ever round up enough people to make patterning happen? Obviously, Dale and I and our teenage son couldn't do it alone. We'd have to get a whole regiment of volunteers.

Nobody would have time to come do this on a daily basis. We'd have to form teams for the various days of the week. And some were always going to have schedule conflicts, trips out of town, and the rest. That would mean recruiting even greater numbers of people. It all seemed wildly unrealistic. Maybe I couldn't pull this off after all.

Friends Indeed

Our friends back in Yakima were curious to know how our trip had gone. I told them about the patterning therapy and what it could possibly accomplish. I shared my excitement but also my trepidation that maybe it wasn't realistic on an ongoing basis.

Jacquie Wonner was one of those listening carefully. She told me later, "In that moment, it was almost as if the Lord whispered, *You're it! You can do this scheduling that Leone needs.*" Jacquie, a natural organizer, volunteered to start lining up teams. She didn't put out a broadcast appeal in the church bulletin or anything else for the public; instead, she handpicked those she thought would warm to this task and called them individually.

To her delight and mine, the responses were largely positive. People who had been wondering what they could do to help David finally had an answer. They said yes, and Jacquie soon had distinct teams for Monday night, Tuesday night, Wednesday night, Thursday night, Friday afternoon, and Saturday afternoon—a couple of dozen people in all, ranging in age from teens to senior citizens. I couldn't believe it.

I was always present as a team member, handling David's head while the others worked his arms and legs. (For some reason David was touchy about who was in charge of turning his head from side to side, trusting only a few others besides me.) My husband committed himself to the Thursday night group, along with young Steve. Our other son, Bill, was headed for college by now, but he, too, found time to fill in when a regular needed to be absent. The teams quickly bonded into close social groups, laughing and telling stories as they met each week in our garage for the ninety-minute sessions.

Joy Campbell joined the Thursday night team along with two of her sons, Todd and Dean. Joy was surprised at how much of a workout *she* got just moving David's right arm. Bill, her husband, often came along to play his natural role as a cutup, cracking jokes and causing distractions. One evening he flagged down the ice cream truck that was circling our neighborhood and bought ice cream for us all. Thereafter, whenever David heard the tinkling music of the ice cream truck, he would lock up his joints and refuse to keep patterning! He wanted a treat instead of all this exertion.

On another occasion, Bill showed up in a new Corvette he had just purchased.

"Hey, Dave—wanna go for a ride in my 'Vette?" he asked.

David immediately broke out in a huge smile and began pumping the air with his thumbs-up signal. I took note of the fact that his brain had readily recognized the meaning of the word *'Vette*. It was another encouraging sign of his language-processing ability.

We loaded David into the sports car, and the two of them took off in a squeal of rubber, zooming toward the boulevard. When they returned, David was squealing with delight of his own.

Debbie Page was another woman from church who agreed to help on the Wednesday night team, along with her six-foot-three son, Brandt, a football player and weight lifter. We assigned Brandt to work David's right leg, the stiffest of all his limbs. Debbie was a fairly new Christian at the time, and she commented to me after a while that she really appreciated spending these evenings in the company of people with more mature faith. She learned a lot from listening to the conversation.

Occasionally she and Brandt would have a typical mother-son disagreement—and we were all amazed to realize that David noticed this. He held a special affinity for Debbie, and whenever the bickering would start, David would begin to mutter, "No! No!" and would lock up his right leg as stiff as a steel beam. Brandt, for all his muscle, could not budge it.

The whole workout would come to a halt until Brandt would apologize by saying, "Okay, Mom—I'm sorry." Then David would let us begin to pattern him once again.

On the other hand, during jovial conversation, there was an opposite complication. If David began laughing too hard at the stories, he couldn't help by relaxing his limbs. Once again, we'd have to sit down and take a break. It was the same with certain trigger words we learned to avoid: "Hawaii," or "Pastor Wayne." If we said either of these, David would lose all focus on the task at hand. During these intervals, I'd bring out coffee or sometimes a snack for everyone.

Real Progress

Patterning became our main strategy for the next four years. We laid aside some of the heavier procedures we'd been using in the garage because we began seeing so much progress through patterning. David's first achievement was tummy crawling—the kind of thing soldiers do in basic training when they scoot along under low-strung barbed wire, propelling themselves only by their elbows. What a day that was to see our son actually get from point A to point B in this manner!

Around the six-month mark came what Florence Scott termed *homolateral crawling*, where he got up on his elbows and knees, and the arm and leg on one side moved forward in sync—first the left side, then the right. Crawling from room to room during the day became easier for David and allowed him to put into practice what the patterning was implanting in his brain. When he needed to use the bathroom, he could crawl there on his own, then kneel at the toilet. If he wanted to go outside onto the patio on a warm day, he could get there without his wheelchair.

I fitted him with knee pads to ease his joints as he kept up with his work. By the time another six months had passed, he was doing cross-lateral crawling, in which the left arm and right leg move forward together, then the right arm and left leg. Again, we watched with astonishment. "David, you're ter-rific!" we would cheer. "You're making so much headway. We're proud of you!"

In time, he even conquered the challenge of crawling up a

set of stairs. This was a great help, since our only bathtub was on the second floor.

And all the exertion had a further benefit: It helped keep his weight under control.

The demand on the patterning teams was not a small one, and one might think that our volunteers would have burned out and dropped away after a while. But their steadfastness was amazing. Jacquie had almost no fill-in recruiting to do. Even the three teenage guys hung steady for the long haul. I got tears in my eyes one Friday afternoon when Glen Laney, a neighbor of ours who was then in his seventies, said, "I have to go into the hospital next week for surgery—they're going to take out one of my kidneys. But I don't think I'll miss more than two weeks of patterning. I should be back here three weeks from today."

Another elderly man, Ron Ewald, came faithfully even though his hands ached from carpal tunnel syndrome. I'm sure the patterning work only made matters worse for him. He, too, took a short break for surgery on his wrists—and then quickly returned to the team. This was the body of Christ at work, its members reaching out in love and concern to help a fellow member. We were a family in need, and these people saw it as their ministry to lift us up. We became a community, and in fact, David was not the only beneficiary. When others in the group went through hard times of their own, we encouraged each other and prayed together. Every life gets a thunderstorm sooner or later, it seems—not just us. We served one another in love through each of those downpours.

By the spring of 1995, we felt we had achieved as much as patterning could do for David. He was now getting from the floor to the couch unaided, and vice versa. He was moving himself in and out of bed on his own. He had mastered his morning routine entirely: getting up, getting dressed, brushing his teeth, using an electric shaver, getting into his wheelchair and rolling himself up to the breakfast table, pouring a bowl of cereal, adding milk without spilling it, eating his meal, and then moving to the mat for the start of crawling exercises.

These motor improvements, I fully believed, were lapping over into other areas of mental processing too. For example, David could now keep track of the days of the week. He could read from his watch what day it was, and if he wanted to communicate this, he would hold up one finger for Monday, two fingers for Tuesday, and so on. I was mystified for a while whenever it happened to be 6 p.m. as I called him to dinner. He would refuse to come out of his room. Why? Because he knew from his watch that it was time for *Star Trek* on TV!

I chose to celebrate our accomplishments with a victory party for the patterning teams. I invited everyone to our home for a celebration. We lined up against the backyard fence for a group picture (see photo section), with David right in the middle. That picture still chokes me up when I think of how many hundreds of hours they gave. I call it "Love's Hall of Fame."

I had the picture silk-screened onto white T-shirts for each of them, with a Scripture quotation from 1 Corinthians 13:13: "And now these three remain: faith, hope and love. But the greatest of these is love." I also managed to get the Yakima City Council to pass a resolution in their honor and give each of them a certificate for their community service.

Imperfect but Still Valuable

Through all this time, we had continued to check back with Florence Scott's clinic in Oregon for updates and further instruction, returning with David every three to four months.

I asked her on one visit, "Say, do you know what ever happened to that little boy who was featured in the *Look* magazine article?"

"Yes, I do," Florence answered. "He grew up to become a successful businessman today. He's fine. That's the benefit of being young when you have a brain injury. The brain hasn't entirely settled on what parts are going to do what, so it can reorganize itself more readily."

Additional progress was made through water therapy. Sharon Crowell, acquatic director at the YMCA, had known David since he was a small boy. "I just know he could benefit from our program," she kept telling me, until I finally enrolled him in the spring of 1993. I convinced him that the water wouldn't be as cold as he remembered from earlier attempts. Soon David was walking back and forth across the pool all by himself.

One young man who helped David in and out of the pool was Paul Dressel, a head-injury victim himself. He had suffered a terrible auto crash as a result of racing away from the police while on drugs, and he still suffered occasional seizures that prevented his driving. But he would meet us at the pool to assist in any way he could. He also walked the eight or so blocks to our house every day for at least two years, spending three hours each day helping David with everything from speech therapy to eye exercises to stretching on the mat. He knew more than any of us what brain damage was all about.

Paul had wonderfully turned his life around and now gave talks to high school students about the dangers of drugs.

About this same time, the Washington State Head Injury Foundation began asking if I would conduct workshops for other parents in similar straits. I agreed to try. With Joy and Bill Campbell's help, I put together a fifty-eight-page handout that told our story, complete with pictures, and drove home the need for families of brain-injury patients to keep seeking options. I told them that if we had given up and parked David in a nursing home, it would have cost the taxpayers of Washington at least $170,000 by now, and he would almost certainly have become a vegetable in diapers, paralyzed and mute. I preached the value of patterning, of course.

Across the state, from Ellensburg to Wenatchee to Mount Vernon (near Puget Sound) and even to Coupeville on Whidbey Island, I gave presentations as part of the foundation's LIFT (Life Initiatives Family Training) program. I got to meet a lot of wonderful, courageous people. We encouraged each other and reinforced the fact that we were not alone in our uphill push against the ravages of brain damage.

We talked about popular misconceptions in society and how to overcome them. Hollywood movies, for example, occasionally employ the head-injury plot for dramatic effect. One such film in the early nineties was *Regarding Henry*, with Harrison Ford and Annette Bening. Ford plays the part of an arrogant defense attorney who is shot in the head and chest during a robbery and slips into a coma. Three weeks later, he awakes with no ability to speak, walk, or remember. Therapy eventually restores his capabilities, and he even emerges gentler and kinder than before.

That's a nice story—but in real life, it usually doesn't work out that cleanly. Those of us who live with the aftermath of a head injury appreciate the media attention, but we want people to know that it's a long, hard, painful road, and families seldom get their loved ones back in original form. We come to learn, however, that even small improvements can be a source of joy. A life does not have to be perfect to be valuable.

I found that the longer we worked with the realities of David's situation, the more I needed to nurture my relationship with God. I began attending a community-wide women's group called Bible Study Fellowship (BSF). More than three hundred women came each week to hear an amazing Spirit-filled teacher, Barbara Dibbert, work through a book of the Bible one chapter at a time. BSF also required extensive homework on the part of the members. As I dug into my workbook and Bible text each week, it fed me spiritually. BSF became an oasis in my week. I'm still there today, more than a decade later.

So many times, what I'm going through in a particular week tracks amazingly with the content of that week's BSF lesson. This is just one way God provides for his people. When we go through trials, he somehow manages to get his message through to us, using various channels.

BSF helped press home to me the meaning of such Scriptures as "He said to me, 'My grace is sufficient for you, for my power is made perfect in weakness.' . . . For when I am weak, then I am strong" (2 Corinthians 12:9-10). Any teaching about the final resurrection brought tears to my eyes as I thought about the truth that someday David's body will be whole again.

Another source of input in the early years was a wonderful retired minister named Chet Dyer, who committed himself to come read the Bible to David once a week. No one knew for sure if David could understand him or not. But that didn't matter to Chet. He believed so strongly in the power of the Word of God that he came like clockwork to provide it. David would sit on the couch and quietly listen, like a grandson listening to his grandfather. After a while, David began to show small signs of response, getting excited at dramatic points in the story Chet was reading.

Meanwhile, I began planning to fold laundry nearby during this time so I could get in on the reading myself. I gained as much from the oral delivery of God's Word as anyone. Chet knew how much I love Psalm 121, so on most days he would say before finishing, "And of course, David, before I go we have to read your mother's favorite psalm!" Then would come the familiar words of comfort:

> I lift up my eyes to the hills—
>   where does my help come from?
> My help comes from the LORD,
>   the Maker of heaven and earth.

Chet Dyer passed away in 1999, after reading the Bible to David and me more than three hundred times. Before he died, he had requested that David be one of the honorary pallbearers at his funeral. The service was a full military funeral, and it was an incredible honor to see Steve pushing David's wheelchair alongside the other pallbearers.

Special events also played a role in bolstering our family's spiritual reserve. One year our church paid the cost for us to go to a special five-day Joni and Friends Family Retreat on the Oregon coast. This gathering of parents and children with disabilities was led by Joni Eareckson Tada, the famous quadriplegic speaker, author, and painter.

I'll never forget watching Joni move through the group in her motorized wheelchair handing out affirmation right and left. "Come on, Dave, let's go down to the beach!" she called at one point. Staff helpers jumped in to do what it took to maneuver Joni and our son, plus others, on an excursion to the waterfront.

Teaching sessions ranged from the inspirational to the very practical. Our friend Dr. Heath had come down from the Tacoma area to conduct some of the classes; it was great to see him again. I sat soaking in the help—but also looking around the room at families that had it worse than we did. It was almost bittersweet to see a young husband caring for his wife, who had been paralyzed from the neck down in a car accident . . . another couple with a baby born with spina bifida. . . . I had to admit that our case was hardly the most severe of the lot. Yet we were all hanging on to the life we had, seeking to make the best of our circumstances as God enabled us.

Times such as these reinforced the truth of the Bible verse on the garage wall back home: "They that wait upon the LORD shall renew their strength. . . ."

Juggling Act

Such inner stamina was essential, because I never knew when life would throw a new challenge my way. One Friday afternoon

I was in the middle of the patterning session when the garage phone rang.

It was my eighty-seven-year-old father calling from Hood River, Oregon. Dad had been a loving and encouraging father in whatever my sister and I tried to do. He had become a Christian at age seventy and had seemingly overcome his drinking problem. But now, his tone was desperate.

"Leone," he said in a slurred voice, "you'd better come down here in a couple days—and you're not going to like what you see." Click—the line went dead.

Oh no. "Dad! Are you still there?!" I shouted into the phone. There was no response.

I instantly redialed his number. Fortunately, he picked up.

"Dad, what do you mean? What are you talking about?" I asked.

"It's too late, Leone. I've already taken 'em." And again, the line went silent.

My heart began pounding. "Excuse me," I said to the patterning group. "I have to quit now." Turning toward the house, I called, "Dale! Can you come take my place?"

I then ran inside and dialed information to get the police department in Hood River, a small town on the Columbia about two and a half hours from us. I blurted out my problem, only to be told that I needed to call the fire department instead.

"I have a crisis on my hands!" I said as soon as I got a response. "My dad—he's eighty-seven years old—lives way out in the country, and he may have taken some pills to end his life. Please go find him! Break down the front door if you have to!"

They asked for directions, which I gave, and soon they were

on their way. When they arrived, the front door was unlocked, and my mother was nowhere to be found. Dad, true to his feisty character, gave them a hard time about getting on the gurney, but by the time they drove him to the hospital, he was in a complete coma.

By then, I was already on the highway to Hood River. My sister likewise began driving from the Seattle area. We arrived to find him still unconscious, his lungs filling with fluid. Suddenly it was déjà vu for me. I was once again sitting in a hospital ICU watching over an unresponsive loved one. *Oh, God,* I silently prayed, *what do we do now? I know Dad would not want to go out like this. Have mercy on him, please.*

On the third day he woke up, and in time he was able to go back home again. The story had a happy ending; he's never again done something drastic like this. He and my mother now live in an assisted-care apartment here in Yakima, calmly enjoying life in their nineties and looking forward to seeing David whenever we bring him over.

Moments such as these may threaten to push us over the edge. But the grace of the Lord is stronger than any emergency—or combination of emergencies. He carries us through when we think we can't stand anymore. He loves us and our family members as much as we do—even more so—and he is our tower of stability through every storm.

Part of his way is to use other people to hold us up. For instance, our son Bud and his wife, Lori, even after moving to Vancouver, Washington (just across the bridge from Portland), would come get David from time to time.

One night while staying there, David rolled out of bed in the middle of the night. Bud awoke to hear a low voice downstairs calling, "Mom . . . Mom . . . Mom." He got up, descended to the ground floor, and there found his brother trapped with his head inside the computer printer table! David had crawled in the dark until he hit an impasse. Bud laughed as he quickly set him free and returned him to his bed.

I heard other such tales of adventure when David got home from these trips. Bud took him once to see the Portland waterfalls, where the walkways are fairly steep. From the spray of the falls, they can also be slippery. Bud was carefully edging David's wheelchair down a slope when, of all times, one rubber tire came off its rim. Bud applied the brakes and then got to work forcing the tire back on, with David's weight still in the chair—not an easy task.

Other outings, however, went far more smoothly. Barry Reifel, a football coach at East Valley High School who attended our church, came by several times in the early 1990s to take David to wrestling matches at the school. Whenever David knew this was on the schedule, he could hardly contain himself in anticipation.

They would usually arrive on campus early so Barry could give him a rolling tour of the halls David once walked as a student. David's face would glow at the sight of familiar classrooms, lockers, and the cafeteria.

"Okay, Dave, it's time to get over to the gym now," Barry said one night. "The match is about to start."

David began vigorously pointing down yet another hallway as if to say, *Not yet! Take me down there too!*

Once in the gym, Barry parked the wheelchair right at the end of the bleachers in a high-traffic lane, with wrestlers constantly going in and out of the dressing rooms. Dozens of people recognized him and stopped to say hi. The look on David's face conveyed his absolute delight at being back in the middle of the action.

Whenever David would come home from one of the trips, he would be completely wired. The laughing and squealing told me I'd better brace myself for a long stretch of trying to calm him down for sleeping.

While friends such as Barry Reifel were serving David directly, other assistance was coming from our attorney, Lou Delorie. He helped us understand that we did have a reasonable claim for damages against the driver of the car that had slowed down in front of David that morning in 1989. "He was preparing to make an illegal left turn, having missed the spot where he should have turned in the first place," Lou explained. "I think we can win this one."

I had already tried, to no avail, to get a workers' compensation settlement, since David was on his way to his job when the accident occurred. The Washington State Department of Labor and Industries had ruled that if he had clocked in at the Pullman store first that morning, then traveled in the direction of the Lewiston store, it could have been viewed as an on-the-job accident. Or if it had occurred in, say, the parking lot of the Pullman store, the same conclusion could have been reached. But since he was coming directly from his apartment to work in Lewiston and the accident occurred on the open highway, no such claim existed.

But what about a claim against the driver's insurance? We had found out that the policy provided $100,000 in liability coverage. "Of course, your expenses have been far greater than that," one of Lou's senior partners commented during a meeting. "This guy may have property or other assets, on top of the insurance."

"No, I don't want to do that," I replied. "I don't want to strip anybody of their home. Whatever we can get from insurance is fine—but that's it."

In late 1992, the $100,000 settlement came through. Lou's firm took a third of it for their professional fees. The State of Washington collected another third in light of all the Medicaid claims they had covered in the early months, which was only fair. The final third came to us. We used it to pay down some of our mortgage, since our home was now also David's home for the foreseeable future.

Money, of course, could never make up for what we had lost. But we chose not to focus on that. One thing we had learned by now was that pining away for losses is just a waste of energy. Far better to think about what we can regain. We got up each day eager to see what new skill or understanding David would acquire on his way forward. We would face the future with optimism and hope.

NINE

Steadily Forward

The end of formal patterning in 1995 did not mean the end of therapy or workouts, by any means. We backed off the intensity a notch, but we certainly had not "arrived." We hoped to see much more progress in mobility, speech, and understanding. "You're going to keep getting better," I told David incessantly. "The more we work, the more we'll find out how much you can achieve." He would smile and nod as he softly replied, "Keep working . . . keep working."

Each day we would spend time crawling. We did a great deal of climbing up and down stairs. We kept using the parallel bars in the garage to improve his gait. I also worked with him on recognizing letters of the alphabet at random, although this tended to frustrate him; eventually I relaxed on that.

As time went on, the boys of the family gradually resumed their fun-loving horseplay of years gone by. Bud, Rob, and Bill got beyond worrying about David's condition and began to find ways to spice up his life. Bill took him one day for an outing to Boulder Cave, some forty miles northwest of Yakima in the Snoqualmie National Forest. It's rugged country, and the trail along the creek that runs through the cave is far from level. Bill came close to dumping his brother out of the wheelchair more than once. I'm glad I wasn't there.

"We had a great time!" Bill reported when they got back. The look on David's face, however, told me he had been truly afraid as they went tilting back and forth down the trail. This excursion had been more daredevil than he wanted.

On another occasion, Bill took David up into the mountains to a favorite campground near where Dale and the boys often went hunting. They were enjoying the high country until it was time to come home again, and Bill found that his car's fuel pump had failed. The afternoon sun was edging lower, and there he was, stuck with his disabled brother far from civilization. This was before cell phones were popular, and in such a remote area, wireless signals might not have reached anyway.

Bill ran to a stranger who was packing up his motor home to leave. "Can you help me out of a jam?" he pleaded. "My car's broken down, and my brother's here with me in a wheelchair—would you call my other brother Rob when you get to Yakima and tell him to come get us? Here's his number. Please?"

The man looked at Bill as if he didn't particularly want to be bothered. But in the end he agreed to pass on the message. A couple of hours passed. Then to Bill's great relief, Rob's truck came rumbling through the woods as daylight was fading.

"Mom, you should have seen it," Rob told me the next day. "Bill had pitched his camping tent just in case it started to rain, and there was David sitting right in the middle of it, having a good time regardless! He didn't appear to have a worry in the world. We carried him back to my truck and then started down the mountain, towing Bill's car—no problem."

I'm glad I only heard about it later.

I was far happier to be on the scene the day my niece Lisa Turner was married to her husband, Jeff—with David as one of the groomsmen. It deeply touched our whole family that Lisa asked her brain-injured cousin to be in the wedding. He looked so nice in his gray tuxedo with all the other attendants, smiling broadly for the camera from his wheelchair. I still look at those pictures and give thanks for a family that didn't want to hide him in a closet somewhere. They reached out to include him in the festivities, making a memory for us all.

Our friends made a point of including him too. They didn't fade away as the years wore on. The Campbells took David out in their van one December night to look at Christmas lights. The highlight of the trip, they said, was one brightly decorated house where the home owner dressed up as Santa and came out to dance a jig whenever cars slowed down in front. David thought this was hilarious.

Elmer Schilperoort, an asparagus farmer whose wife had worked with me at JCPenney, came by a number of times to take David out in one of his old classic cars. Elmer's collection included a Studebaker, a bubble-top Mercedes, and a DeSoto that still carried the markings of the California Highway Patrol.

But David's favorite was his yellow 1965 Mustang. David's face would just glow whenever he got to ride in this car, not only for the automobile lore it represented, but because he knew Elmer would always stop along the way for a hamburger, fries, and a milk shake.

On one excursion, Elmer stopped at the home of his cousin, who invited them to come inside. This meant getting David out of the car and into his wheelchair. Elmer pulled the bulky apparatus out of the Mustang trunk and rolled it up to the passenger-side door. But David wouldn't get into the chair.

"Come on, David—they want us to go inside for a bit," Elmer coaxed. David wouldn't budge. He kept motioning to the chair, then to the back of the car, then to the chair again, a scowl on his face. His grunts meant something was wrong, although he couldn't articulate what it was.

Several minutes went by as Elmer scratched his head. Then he finally unraveled the mystery. The black foam-rubber seat cushion, which attached by Velcro to the wheelchair canvas, was missing! Once Elmer retrieved this piece from the trunk and put it in place, David was happy to cooperate once again. He swung right out of the car and into his spot.

Another old-car fan was Ed Cunnington, David's favorite band teacher from high school days, nicknamed "the Boss." Ed stopped by with his ancient yellow Chevrolet convertible to brighten Dave's day more than once.

Other friends brought their love and attention to our house. After Chet Dyer, who read the Bible to David, passed away and no longer came to read the Bible to David, Jacquie Wonner took up the reading mantle. She began stopping by on her lunch hour from work to read David an assortment of materials. She brought a newsletter from Brother Andrew, the adventurous Dutch missionary who was then taking the *JESUS* film into risky places. Some of the stories were downright miraculous. David would listen intently, and as the climax of the story would near, his excitement would mount. There was no question he was tracking with her narrative.

If a story involved physical violence, however, he would begin to frown and protest. He didn't want to hear that part, it seemed.

Somehow Jacquie figured out that David had a special love for eagles—perhaps from the Isaiah 40 Scripture on the inside of the garage door ("They shall mount up with wings as eagles"). At a yard sale she found a book about eagles with many colorful pictures. She read David this book from start to finish over a number of weeks.

Her reading visits went on for at least two years. She claimed she enjoyed it, and we were certainly grateful.

The biggest weekly highlight for David was going to church each Sunday. People greeted him warmly in the lobby, both on the way in and when leaving at the end. For the service, we parked his wheelchair at the end of a row near the back, and as soon as the music started, his animation level would jump. His head would bob up and down to the rhythm, and his arms would sway as well. If he really liked a certain song, he'd reach out and give me a playful punch in the arm, as if to convey, "This is really a good one!" On the other hand, if the music got *too* contemporary for his tastes, he would begin to shake his head vigorously.

His love for the Lord was obvious. Choir members told me they almost had to force themselves not to look at his dancing arms and crinkling dimples, or else they would break down. They would focus on a different part of the sanctuary when it was their turn to sing. "If we look at David when we're supposed to be performing, we just lose it," they said.

There was little doubt in my mind that he tracked along with the sermons. Often he would punch my arm in approval when the pastor made a strong point. Sometimes I even had to whisper, "Okay, David, that's enough!" When it was time to pray, he was always among the first to bow his head and tightly close his eyes.

A sad event for David and all of us happened in the fall of 1997, when Pastor Wayne Pickens's tenure at our church came to an end. How we hated to see him go. During his last week in town, before heading to a new pastorate in La Grande, Oregon, he and his wife, Bonnie, stopped by our house to say good-bye. Soon David was motioning for them to follow him as he crawled toward his room. There he opened up his wardrobe (a low cabinet I had found to accommodate his level near the floor) and pulled out a shirt for them to see. "Sunday shirt!" he proudly announced. In his perception, the Pickenses were all about Sunday. He wanted the pastor to see that he was well prepared for the next Lord's Day.

Pastor Wayne complimented him on his shirt and then took time to pray a special prayer for David while standing there in his room. David reached out to grab the pastor's pant leg. We were all teary by the time the Pickenses headed out the door that day. Now several years have passed, but any mention of Pastor Wayne still gets an energetic response from David. He will never forget the shepherd who cared for him through his terrible ordeal.

Setback

The next year, 1998, we suffered an interruption in our pursuit of progress for David—and it was mainly my fault. His right leg had always been the stiffest, due no doubt to the left-side brain surgery in the beginning. I began discussing with the doctors at Good Samaritan Hospital in Puyallup whether a procedure to lengthen his Achilles tendon might give him more range of motion.

It seemed like a good thing to try. We set the date, and David came through the surgery in fine shape.

The outcome, however, was not what we had hoped for. His right foot soon began to turn outward as a result of the loosened tendon. This caused more dragging of the foot. The muscles in the right calf seemed to atrophy. We had traded one limitation for another.

I felt bad about my decision. But it had seemed right at the time, and the only thing we could do now was to keep working with the leg as it was, trying to build up strength and control through tons of stretching exercises. To this day, we are still working to get the right leg in gear with the left.

Our setback was nothing compared to that of a courageous single mom in town I met named Cindy Hart. On a foggy January morning in 1994, her fourteen-year-old son, Adam, started to dash across Tieton Drive on his way to school but never made it to the other side of the avenue. He ran full speed into a car, sustaining massive brain damage.

Eight months later, Adam came out of his coma. Soon thereafter, Cindy started patterning, having seen David's progress and consulted with Florence Scott. She managed to get enough helpers to pull it off, many of them through the karate school where Adam had been so successful. The day Adam lifted his head off the mat, held it up, and looked around the room, everyone was ecstatic. He was so motivated to crawl that he would even dig his chin into the floor to help propel himself forward. Speech therapists, meanwhile, got him to blink his eyes for yes and shake his head for no. Soon the stomach feeding tube would be removed, it seemed. Our newspaper ran a large photo feature on Adam one Sunday entitled "A Pattern of Hope."

Then one day in 1997, Adam began having heart problems. At the hospital, during a procedure to reintroduce a tracheal tube, Adam aspirated some of the stomach's acidic fluid into his lungs. Suddenly, he was in respiratory crisis. The only way to keep supplying the necessary oxygen was to put the young man, now seventeen years old, on a ventilator.

I wept with Cindy as we stood by his bed and grieved the loss of earlier hopes. She brought Adam home—ventilator and all—to care for him in his grave condition. Any rehab—patterning or otherwise—was now impossible. She still hoped and prayed for his improvement, but all signs pointed the other direction. Over the next few years, he developed juvenile diabetes and lost all his toenails. Would amputations soon follow?

Then one morning in July 2000, she called me with an odd message. "Um, I was just wondering if you might like to have Adam's standing table," she said, referring to the therapy apparatus that helps patients stand vertical.

"Why?" I responded. "What are you saying?"

"Well . . . I'm thinking of letting him go."

I was the older mom here, who had been coping with a

head-injured son much longer than she had. I knew she looked up to me. I weighed my next words carefully. I said, "Cindy, I really think God has been trying to take Adam home for a long time. You have given him your absolutely best effort—110 percent. You've done everything for Adam you possibly could. We're getting nowhere now; there are not even tiny hints of a comeback, no indication that he'll ever get off the ventilator.

"In such a situation, I'm not a diehard or an absolutist. I think you'd be justified in turning off the machines. And if you do, you should have no regrets."

She began to cry. We talked a bit longer, and soon after she spoke with her doctor to convey her decision.

Some two dozen of us—family members, friends, her pastor, a worker from Providence Hospice—gathered at her house that summer morning just a few days after Adam's twenty-first birthday to be with her as she compassionately and lovingly allowed her only son to head for eternity. The dying process was neither pretty nor swift; it took another five days, during which time Cindy kept putting ice chips in his mouth to relieve his thirst.

I tell this sad story to illustrate that not every trauma in life can be recouped. In writing this book, I do not mean to imply that every head injury or other catastrophe will turn out as well as David's. We ought to give it our fullest effort, of course, standing strong in hope and courage. As long as the medical prognosis is mixed or even cloudy, we must hold to the side of life. But when it becomes obvious that we've lost the battle, it's not wrong to admit it—even though it rips a mother's heart in two.

Life Goes On

As the years passed, I kept doing what mothers do, which is to get up morning after morning and care for their children. David remained content, and I disciplined myself to live in the present, not the past.

I've been tempted at times to get off on a nostalgic trip, recalling the energetic young man David used to be in high school and college. He even had the nickname "Super-Dave" in those days, because he always seemed to be flying about six feet off the ground. I could mourn for what would never develop. That would soon lead to a grumbling in my spirit against God and to unanswerable questions about why he had allowed the accident to happen.

It was far more healthy, however, to stay in the moment. Whenever there was a small sign of progress—a new word out of his mouth, for example, or a little more endurance for some physical challenge—I could rejoice. I certainly had plenty to do, organizing David's every activity. This was a full-time job, to be sure.

I counted myself fortunate that my husband had an equal measure of stick-to-the-task determination. I don't know what I would have done if Dale had been one of those men who always wanted to take off for the weekend, head for a time-share on the beach, or whatever. He was as much a workaholic as I was. In fact, we'd never taken much of a vacation in the ten years of married life *before* David's accident. We just naturally kept our noses to the grindstone.

People who read about a head injury in the newspaper or see it on the evening news, I've noticed, react with an "Oh my goodness, that's really awful"—but don't comprehend the permanent change it brings to a family's life. They go on to the next article, the next news feature, and forget about it. I'm not being critical; this is an understandable reaction. But when you're living it day after day, month after month, year after year, it's a whole different experience.

One reality is that brain damage more or less cancels all internal sense of "hurry up." The patient has no sense of time or deadline and thus no impetus to get moving. All this has to be imposed from the outside.

I fully admit there have been times when I've neglected my other boys while absorbed in David's needs. Dale has no doubt felt left out as well sometimes. It's not the normal way for a family to function. I've been obsessed with the work at hand, to the point of exhaustion. I will always be thankful for how the guys have flexed with me and given me slack—everything from fixing their own lunches to putting up with my lack of full attention to their concerns.

Bud, my oldest, was already out of the house when David got hurt. But in a different vein, Bud had his own struggle. Not long ago, he recounted it this way: "Way back when I was no more than six years old and Dad [meaning Leo] was being so hard on us, I think I figured out that there was a light side to this world and a dark side. Dad, with all his drinking and violent behavior, was part of the darkness. I chose the light side.

"Through many, many episodes and challenges, God was the strength I needed as a kid to stay on the side of the light. He loved me, cared about me, and was my hope for protection.

"Then came David's accident. It was so random, so unexplainable—and so permanent. *What happened to God's protection from the darkness?* I asked myself."

Bud stopped talking for a moment, then continued. "It took me seven or eight years to realize that God's main role in our lives is not to shield us from trouble. He walks with us *through* our trouble. Yes, he listens to our prayers, and he does intervene at times. But primarily, he sustains us *in the middle of* our dark circumstances.

"A lot of people in the world get mad at God because he didn't protect them from a particular trial. But that isn't his major role. Instead, it is to hold us close in spite of the storm that rages all around. It's a whole change of perspective."

That has certainly been my experience as well. Day after day, God enables me to do the job at hand. As I live and function in the present, he is there to get me through.

Meanwhile, the calendar keeps turning. One Sunday morning in 2001, I saw Dr. Bracchi at church and said, "You know what? I haven't brought David in for a general checkup in ten years! He's just been going along in his normal way. Do you think you ought to see him again?" (I feared he thought we'd switched to another doctor.)

"Yes, that would probably be a good idea," Dr. Bracchi replied.

So we made an appointment for a full physical. Again, the results were stable. Nothing needed further attention. David was doing well.

Sometime later, however, I noticed my son seemed a bit agitated. His head seem to bob around abnormally.

"Are you okay, David?" I asked him. "Is anything wrong?"

"Weird," he replied. "Weird. Feel weird."

That was a new word in his vocabulary. I didn't know what it signified but decided I'd better take him back to Dr.

Bracchi's office. There the doctor discovered that he had an abundance of earwax ("enough to grow potatoes!" the nurse said), which was messing up his sense of balance. No wonder he felt "weird."

This was one of the first times David had succeeded in identifying, even in general terms, the nature of a physical ailment. I chose to view this as another step forward in mental processing. The old myth that head-injury patients recover as much functionality as they ever will within two years of their trauma was again disproved.

TEN

Planning for the Future

A quiet, perplexing question hovered in the air during these years, unspoken for the most part except when Dale and I would linger over a cup of coffee or lie awake in bed talking at night: *What's going to happen to David when we can't keep caring for him?* After all, I had to admit I was edging closer and closer to my sixties, and Dale was already there.

I had no health problems at the present, for which I was most thankful. I could still put in full days of managing David's life, pushing him through his workouts and maintaining a household that included a disabled adult. I didn't mind the lifestyle at all, even if a lot of women my age now had more time to pamper themselves, whether by getting a manicure or roaming the mall. Here I was, by contrast, completely absorbed in the needs of a thirtysomething toddler.

In terms of physical stamina, however, both Dale and I knew that our days of doing round-the-clock care were numbered. We had to think about the future.

"What if we set him up in his own place and hired a caregiver to stay with him?" I said to Dale one morning. He looked at me as if I'd lost my mind. "No, I'm serious," I continued. "He's really able to take care of a lot of his basic functions. And let's face it: He can't live with us forever, because we're not going to *be here* forever!"

"Well, you're right about that one," my husband admitted. "But you're talking about a lot of money here. How would we ever pull this off financially?"

We began tallying up the available resources. David was getting $557 a month from Social Security as a disabled adult, based on his early earnings back in the JCPenney days. We could pull out the $33,333 of insurance settlement money from the accident that we had applied to our house equity, plus appreciation. This would in essence buy out his "share" so he could then reinvest it in a place of his own.

I proposed to Dale that we look for some kind of multiunit property so that David could live in one part and we could rent out the rest to pay the mortgage. We'd certainly have to borrow more cash to make this work. But if the rental stream was adequate, it could keep up with the mortgage plus taxes, insurance, and maintenance.

We knew from past investigation that state funds would pay for a live-in caregiver. But how would we ever find one who would do a conscientious job, as opposed to just sitting around? We didn't know where to start.

We mused back and forth about all this for a long time. We

did research. We talked to the rest of the family. We didn't always agree. Bud and Lori encouraged us to think about adult foster care instead of taking all the responsibility on ourselves to set David up in his own place. At times, Dale and I simply did not see eye to eye, which created tension. We'd get into little spats about entirely different subjects, it seemed, when what was really causing the irritation was the matter of David's future. The boys noticed this, I'm sure.

I prayed that if this plan was workable, God would guide our steps. I began browsing the real estate ads. Eventually, I contacted a buyer's agent. The very first place we went to see—a duplex on Cedar Hills Court near the end of a cul-de-sac—was absolutely perfect. Each unit had a combination living room–kitchen that was nice and airy, wide hallways to accommodate a wheelchair, two bedrooms and two full baths, plus a one-car garage that we could make into a workout space as we'd done at our own house. The street was quiet, and there was a shade tree growing in front. The price for the whole property: $151,000.

Little did I know at the time that across the street lived Cara Anderson, the rehab nurse who had done so much for David back in 1990! She was the one who had pleaded with Dr. Bracchi to come make his own independent assessment, which opened the door to all kinds of good things. We didn't discover that she was a neighbor until later.

We scraped together what money we could, then went to the bank and got a mortgage to buy the place. Renters currently occupied the two units, so we couldn't actually move David in until at least one lease ran out. That was all right; we had other work to do in the meantime. Inside, I was thrilled at the prospects for David. We were starting down a road that would secure his future indefinitely.

Details, Details

One of the things we learned was that if we put the entire property in David's name, that would make him a landlord in the eyes of the government, with rental money coming in—which would jeopardize his Medicaid insurance. The rules said that anyone with more than two thousand dollars in assets (beyond a home and a vehicle) would be disqualified for assistance.

As mentioned in a previous chapter, Medicaid was absolutely essential for David; no other health insurer would even think about taking him in his present condition. What to do?

A financial counselor introduced us to the concept of setting up a trust that would own and manage the other side of the duplex for David's benefit. It took a lot of paperwork, but eventually the David Michael McRae Irrevocable Special Needs Trust came into being. As owner of half of the duplex, the trust could receive all rental income, then pay its half of the mortgage, taxes, and insurance, while also building up a maintenance reserve to put on new gutters or fix the plumbing whenever needed. Meanwhile, David's personal cash would not exceed the two-thousand-dollar ceiling. It sounds complicated—and it is. But it's entirely legal and justified for the purpose of guaranteeing that David will have a roof over his head long after Dale and I are gone.

I got busy looking for furniture. When Dale saw the big queen bed with the mahogany headboard I'd picked out for David, he gasped. "Leone! What are you thinking? That's way too high off the floor for him to get in and out."

"No, it's not," I countered. "He can manage this just fine. Watch him." I brought David in for a demonstration, and sure enough, he hoisted himself up onto the comfy mattress without a problem. He also got back down all right. The smile on his face said he knew this would become his special nest.

Once the renters moved out, we had a great deal of work to do. Rob brought his ladder and got busy with the high painting; Rob's wife, Kim, helped with the open house; and Bill and Steve helped rip out old carpet. Meanwhile, we interviewed various caregivers, eventually selecting one. The momentous day came in 2001 when we finally moved David into his own place. I was overwhelmed with gratitude when I thought about how the Lord had brought us along a very long road. Who would have thought back in the early days, when everything looked so grim, that our head-injured son would someday be able to live on his own? Who would have predicted any kind of viable future for him? Now it was coming to pass.

A Visitor

Two months after move-in day, on an ordinary afternoon, the phone in our kitchen rang. I picked it up, and a woman's voice said, "Hello, I'm calling from Spokane. My name is Linda Sharp. I don't know if you remember me."

The woman who comforted David that awful day on the highway twelve years ago! "I will never forget your name!" I cried, bursting into tears.

"I've never forgotten you, either," she replied. "Tell me about David these days. I keep wondering about him."

I launched into a detailed description of what he had come through, how much the patterning therapy had helped him, and how well he was doing presently. "In fact, you won't believe this, but we've just moved him into his own place!"

"Well, I'm so glad to hear that," Linda replied. "I don't know if you ever knew that back in '89, after a few weeks I drove down to the Lewiston hospital again to check up on him. And you all had already transferred him to Yakima by then. So I was left wondering.

"A few months into the new year, I got a job at a bank in Pullman where a lot of WSU students came in. Every time I'd see a Yakima address on somebody's deposit slip, I'd ask if they knew anything about David McRae. Most of the kids said no. But then one guy said he thought he'd seen a newspaper article about him coming out of his coma or something. That's all I had to go on."

"Oh, Linda, you did such a wonderful thing for him that terrible day!" I interrupted. "And the truth is, if you hadn't called me back then to say that the accident was not his fault, we would never have followed up. We wouldn't have gotten the insurance settlement—and he never would have been able to afford this duplex. It all started with you!"

"Wow, that is amazing," she said. "I was just wondering, would you care if I came to see him sometime?"

"That would be terrific," I replied. "Let's find a date."

The day this dark-haired woman, along with her teenage daughter, Katie, showed up at David's place was extremely emotional. I swept her into my arms as I cried, "Thank you so very much!"

David, of course, had no working memory of the role she had played in his life. But he was pleasant, as usual, when she came to greet him. We sat talking for a long time, catching up on all that had transpired. She was so pleased to see him living in his own quarters and getting along so well.

I had arranged for Cara Anderson to come across the street and meet Linda as well. We posed the two of them with David in the front yard for a picture (see photo section).

Before she left that day, Linda said quietly, "You know, whenever we drive down to Lewiston even today, the car gets real quiet at that intersection. Katie will say to me, 'You're thinking about David, aren't you?' And she's right. It was indeed a life-changing experience for me, one that I'll cherish in my heart for the rest of my life."

I reached out for her hand once again, the hand that had caressed David's face as he lay on the double yellow line. Katie looked on with amazement and pride at her mother.

"I don't mean to boast," Linda continued, "but the ambulance driver told me when I talked to him on the phone a few days later, 'Linda, what you did probably saved his life. The power of human touch keeps people connected during trauma, even if they're unconscious. Just to feel you touching him is probably what kept him alive until we could get there to pick him up.'"

I replied, "That makes total sense. I truly believe God had someone with a mother's heart to come along at just that moment. I could never repay you enough for what you did for my son."

Trusting the Caregiver

It felt strange in the evenings, I admit, for Dale and me to go to bed in a quiet house, trusting that David and his caregiver would get along all right through the night. I would stop by nearly every day to see how things were going and to give instructions on the therapy program that should continue.

The first man we hired did quite a good job, we felt. He was personable, and David got along well with him. We weren't happy, however, on January 21, 2002, when while transferring from the wheelchair to the commode, David fell and broke the second toe on his right foot. We wanted someone who would pay full attention to his safety at all times.

Subsequent caregivers proved to be a mixed lot. One man, we found out, would put David to bed in the evening and then slip out to spend the night with his girlfriend, returning the next morning to take up his duties once again! We quickly sent him packing. Another woman, whom I'd known for a long time, seemed as if she would be a good fit; she was going through a divorce and needed a place to stay. But eventually we discerned that she had a different agenda for David, hoping to get him enrolled at the handicap workshop in town, where the mentally challenged do routine jobs for various businesses. That wasn't our vision at all.

David, in fact, had his own opinions about caregivers. One time one of them gave him a fairly aggressive haircut that turned out almost like a buzz. When David saw himself in the mirror, he began pointing his finger and saying with great agitation, "You . . . you . . . you . . . you . . . *fired!*" We all just had to laugh.

We truly hit the jackpot, however, when Andre Cadousteau came to work for us in 2003. A Tahitian who had immigrated to the States in 1982, Andre has proved to be a fabulous caregiver, and we trust him implicitly. He's kind, he's diligent, and he is a "gentle slave driver" when it comes to daily therapy.

"Okay, David," he'll say after breakfast each day, "it's time to get to work in the garage." Soon David is pacing back and forth for thirty minutes in the parallel bars. Next he may be pedaling away on the stationary bike, Andre watching carefully to make sure David's weaker right foot doesn't slip. Then comes a stint in a Body by Jake Bun and Thigh Rocker to build up leg strength. Eventually Andre straps him into the standing table, which forces an upright posture; there David works at putting various sizes of dowels in and out of holes in a Peg-Board made for him by Grandpa Funston, my father.

More recently we have gotten so bold as to install a treadmill. Naturally, David does not have enough balance control to be able to stay on the moving belt, but we've rigged up a support harness from a well-secured ceiling hook to keep him in place. The harness is actually the kind rock climbers use when they're belaying one another up and down sheer cliffs. Andre straps David into this, hoists him up just slightly from the belt, and turns on the machine at a slow speed. For the next thirty minutes, David walks steadily, smiling as he huffs and puffs, while Andre monitors his right foot. A *Rocky* poster on the wall lends its inspiration to keep moving and never give up.

When garage time is finished, the work is not yet done. Andre brings David inside the house for floor exercises, or what David refers to as "torture." Again, we brush this off by saying, "Yeah, but it's really good for you. Andre is helping you a lot." Stomach crunches are first, then leg-ups, then knee extensions, as a physical therapist would do. Soon David is positioned in his wheelchair facing the kitchen sink, where he must grab the edge of the counter and pull himself up to a full standing position. The daily quota: five hundred pull-ups.

But there's also time for relaxation and fun in this place. On the coffee table sits an oversize tic-tac-toe game with movable Xs and Os. David has become virtually unbeatable at this. On the wall in a prominent place hangs his JCPenney Customer Service Award plaque, including a photo of him as an energetic eighteen-year-old in a plaid shirt with a tie. David looks at it often and tells anyone who will listen, "One, two, three, four, five!" That means he was a Penney's employee for a total of five years.

Live-in caregivers are asked to work a five-day week, but around the clock. With our current schedule, we pick up David each Wednesday morning to come to our house and return him to Andre on Friday morning. This gives the caregiver a break from responsibility and a chance to pursue personal interests and errands.

Financial Snag

We hit a serious snag in May 2003, when a government bureaucrat, not understanding the provisions of the irrevocable special-needs trust, decided to stop David's benefits. We got a form letter from the state's Department of Social and Health Services that began: "Dear Ms./Mr. David McRae: Your SSI Federal and State cash payments have ended. . . ."

I panicked. David's entire financial viability was being cut off at the knees. We fired off a written protest in response. We reminded the authorities that for thirteen years we had cared for David in our own home, saving the state huge amounts of money in nursing home costs. We were in no way trying to rip off the system; we were simply trying to be foresighted in planning for the future.

Three weeks later we got another form letter informing us that David had already received too much SSI money, specifically, $435.90, and would need to pay Uncle Sam back! This was because, they said, he had stayed at our house from time to time and thus gotten "free food, clothing, and shelter" beyond his normal circumstance. So much for clarifying the picture.

I will spare you all the blow-by-blow details of going back and forth with one official after another over the following months. At one point I took David along in his wheelchair for what turned out to be a three-hour meeting with a certain Social Security Administration caseworker, who shall remain nameless. He had the nerve to sit there looking at a young man who could not walk or even stand unaided and could hardly speak three words in a row—and claim we deserved no assistance.

As a matter of fact, David qualified for even *more* assistance. A friend happened to say to me at one point, "Is David's natural father still alive?" No, Leo McRae had died as a result of complications from his alcoholism in 1999. "Well then," the friend continued, "David deserves child survivor benefits, since he's still unable to support himself."

Wow, I'd never even thought of that. We began checking it out. Sure enough, after some further teeth pulling, a new monthly benefit of $322 began to flow.

By the time the dust settled, I had been in touch with our state representative, the governor's office in Olympia, and even the White House. A high official there in the finance division called me to say that our trust was in full compliance with the law and should in no way jeopardize David's benefits. He must have passed the word along, because in August we received a letter from Crawford, Texas:

Dear Mr. and Mrs. Nunley:

I recently learned about your extraordinary efforts to care for your son David McRae.

The strength and perseverance of your family and friends demonstrate the spirit of our Nation. Laura and I join you in celebrating David's success.

May God bless you and your family.

Sincerely,

George W. Bush

The moral to this saga is that you have to be persistent, not assuming that every statement on government letterhead is correct. If you've done your homework, if you've studied the rules, and if you've put your situation in proper order (for example, our trust), you have a right to insist on fair treatment. That's not being obnoxious or greedy; it's just making sure the system delivers what it was meant to provide: help for those who cannot help themselves, namely, the elderly and the disabled.

Friends Forever

Fortunately during this period, David did not comprehend that he was in financial jeopardy and therefore didn't worry about it. He went on enjoying daily life as always. He's such a social guy that any chance to be with people brought him pleasure.

If he and I were in the car running errands and I whipped into a fast food drive-through lane to get a couple of burgers, he'd show his disappointment by saying, "Go in? Go in?" Why should we sit in the car and eat when we could go in and be with people!

One day he was sitting at the kitchen counter eating a snack with me, when out of the blue, he came up with the phrase "Friends forever!" I have no idea where he got that.

"Yes, David, that's true," I answered. "I'm not only your mother, but I'm your friend forever. We're buds, you and me."

I feel this bond especially when we're on the sidewalk in front of our house, doing his walking regimen. He takes his frame walker and slowly shuffles to the end of the block, then turns around and returns to our corner. I walk alongside him, watching every step, making sure he notices the occasional crack where one slab of concrete is higher than the other and could make him fall. By the end of one trip, he needs to rest in his wheelchair for fifteen minutes or so before starting the next lap. All in all, he's now walking ten blocks a day; the whole process takes two and a half hours. When he is at his own place, Andre has him do the same routine.

People drive by and wave to him, which encourages him all the more. Neighbors out walking their dogs stop to talk. "David, you're doing so well!" they say. He loves the attention.

I take my cordless phone along with me, in case calls come in. When David is resting, I pull weeds in my flower beds; I have one of the better-looking yards in the subdivision for all the time I get to spend outdoors with David. It's never a drag. It's a time to reflect on how far this son has come and to applaud his efforts.

How far will David go in the years to come? My next goal is to switch him from a walker to just a cane for short distances. That would give him even more flexibility. I don't know if it's possible or not, but we're going to give it a try.

On the language front—his area of greatest loss—we'll keep

trying to expand his vocabulary. He currently says about two hundred words. Some of his recent additions have been "golf" when we drive by the golf course, "church" when we arrive at West Side Baptist for a service, and "medi-center" whenever we go by the clinic. I may also start experimenting with simplified sign language; there's some evidence that brain-injured victims can do quite well at signing even when their speech is limited.

In the writing area, we seem to have hit something of a wall. He can correctly make the capital letters *A, B, C, D, E, I, O, S, V, X,* and *Z* upon verbal command, but that list has not expanded in recent years. He can, however, copy anything if I write it out first.

We just may get to a point in the distant future when David could handle overnights alone. The caregiver could leave at seven in the evening, say, and return at eight the next morning. We could rig up an alarm button for him to push if he felt he needed us to drive over and assist him with something. For now, such an arrangement would be dangerous. But in the future, who knows?

From my viewpoint, David is still improving after sixteen years. Though he still has physical limitations, we praise God every day for the miracle of watching him continue to make progress. Dr. Bracchi tells me not to expect a great deal from now on, given the fact that David is getting older. But even he, the ever-cautious physician, adds, "We'll see what happens, won't we? I continue to pray for miracles in this case. We pray for David both in our home and in leadership meetings at church. What God will do is up to God."

That's the tone of our prayer as well: "Lord, please help

David to go as far as you want him to go. Guide us as we serve him, and let his example be an inspiration to everyone who sees him."

The tragedy of David's accident will never be erased, of course. But out of catastrophe, much good has emerged. In the words of Isaiah 61:3, God has seen fit to "bestow on [us] a crown of beauty instead of ashes, the oil of gladness instead of mourning, and a garment of praise instead of a spirit of despair."

This situation has not broken our family. It has, indeed, made us stronger. We look with hope and expectancy toward whatever is yet to come.

ELEVEN

Very Much Alive

When David is at our house and his workouts are finished for the day, I'll often turn on a cable news network for him to watch. If a story is positive, he will sometimes signal his opinion with a thumbs-up. If a story is negative, however, his forehead will crease into a frown as he says, almost with a catch in his throat, "Bad news! Bad news!"

Through the winter of 2004 and early spring of 2005, I started steering David away from the news, as the Terri Schiavo situation began to dominate the airwaves. I didn't want him to realize that another brain-damaged American, just four years older than he, was being ushered steadily toward death.

Upstairs on our bedroom TV, however, the events in Pinellas Park, Florida, had me in their grip. When I saw pictures of Terri taken shortly after her collapse in 1990, I noticed that her head was up, her shoulders were back, her eyes were open, and she wasn't drooling—she didn't even look brain injured. David had looked far worse in the early stages. The contrast between my son, now so vibrant and alive and curious and energized, and the current Terri Schiavo was so striking that I couldn't resist taking action. I began making phone calls.

I boldly dialed the Schindler home and was amazed to get Terri's father on the line right away. I gave a quick description of David's case, and when I got to the part about patterning therapy, he interrupted me.

"Yes, I've heard about that. It originally came out of Philadelphia, didn't it? We used to live in Pennsylvania before we moved down here."

"That's right!" I answered. "It really is a marvelous discovery."

Bob Schindler then volunteered that he was still mystified by what had caused his daughter's collapse. "It's very suspect, very troubling," he said.

I urged him to fight on for his loved one. "God created our brains to be able to reorganize after a trauma, if given therapy and a loving environment," I said. "The amount of recovery varies, of course. But please don't give up."

"We're not giving up," he replied. "That's exactly what we've been trying to tell Michael, her husband, for so long: 'If you want out of this ordeal, okay! Just turn her over to us, her blood family. We'll take up the responsibility, pay the bills, everything. Please give us a chance.' But his mind is made up. He won't even permit flowers in the room. The nurses are forbidden to put a soft washcloth in her hands so they don't clench into tight little fists. It's horrible."

Soon I was on the line to Governor Jeb Bush's office in Tallahassee, making the same plea. I also talked to Florida's department of adult protection services. I called congresspeople in Washington, various media networks, and the Schindler family's lawyer. I even called George Felos, the attorney for Terri's husband, Michael, but couldn't get past the receptionist. She let me know in no uncertain terms that they were not interested in my views. When the phone bill arrived a few weeks later, Dale said, "My goodness, Leone, you've made a hundred long-distance calls!" I hadn't realized it was that many, but they were worth it if Terri's life could be spared.

In all of this, I did not assume that Terri's medical case was the same as David's. Our son had suffered major blunt force trauma to the head by hitting an asphalt roadway; nobody quite knew what had made Terri Schiavo black out that morning in 1990. In fact, we still don't know. Even the autopsy couldn't verify an eating disorder or any of the other various theories.

But the results were eerily similar—a patient lying motionless and unresponsive. When I quizzed Dr. Bracchi about this, he replied, "Well, certainly at the beginning, David's neurological function was no better than hers." The two cases, if not identical, were awfully close. Both patients were declared to be in a "persistent vegetative state" and stayed that way for months. (The term itself, by the way, is less than precise; it leaves room for lots of unknowns—and lots of potential to improve.)

Roxeanne Vainuku of KIMA-TV, the CBS affiliate here in Yakima, called to ask if she could bring a camera crew to our house and talk about the Schiavo controversy. She had done several good features on David in the past, so I readily agreed. "You know what's really sad about all this?" I said on the air. "The family hasn't had a chance. For years they've been shut out of the process.

"So we'll never know, will we? We'll never find out what Terri could have regained. What a lost opportunity."

All across the nation, people were talking and thinking. Mark Galli, managing editor of *Christianity Today*, wrote a thought-provoking list of questions that arose from Terri's case. One in particular caught my attention: "If there are people who were willing and able to take care of Terri, why weren't they allowed to practice such extraordinary love?"[7]

One day in late March I called the Schindler home again. This time I spoke with Terri's sister-in-law. By now the battle was all but lost. "Can't the courts help you get this right?" I asked. "I know you've tried so much, but still—"

"Apparently not," the sister-in-law replied in a despondent voice. "The laws really need to change on this. If the legal guardian doesn't want to keep dealing with the problem, but somebody else is willing to take over, we ought to have a shot."

Beyond the Feeding Tube

Virtually all the media attention focused on Terri's feeding tube: Should it stay in place or be removed? In a way, I suppose David's story illustrates that putting in a feeding tube is much easier than taking it out. Not just for physical reasons, as in our case, but more often for ethical reasons. Once families allow a medical staff to start providing nutrition through a tube, it can be a wrenching decision ever to stop. Granted, when a person is first injured or collapses, a feeding tube is sometimes a necessity; the patient won't live without it. But the sooner it can be removed, the better, and looking back, I'm grateful we pushed to get David eating by mouth as early as we could.

In 2000, the Schindlers had filed a court petition to conduct simple swallowing tests that would determine whether Terri could get nutrition orally instead of by a feeding tube. It was denied by Judge Greer, even after one nursing assistant testified under oath that she had secretly fed Terri "small mouthfuls of Jello, which she was able to swallow and enjoyed immensely."[8]

Actually, while the feeding tube became the focus of the Terri Schiavo debate, to me that was not the main issue. The real tragedy was the withholding of stimulation, therapy, and encouragement all through the years. All rehabilitation efforts basically ceased in 1994, not long after Michael and the Schindlers had a major falling-out. And so this precious young woman was essentially locked up in solitary confinement.

As Dr. Joseph J. Fins, chief of the medical ethics division at New York Weill Cornell Medical Center, told a *Chicago Tribune* reporter, "If you are conscious but are not identified as such, if you're isolated in a nursing home with no meaningful interaction of any kind, you've been exiled from the world." Dr. Jeffrey Frank, director of neurological intensive care at the University of Chicago Hospitals, termed such patients "neurologically abandoned,"[9] even though they are very much alive.

No wonder, then, the autopsy showed that Terri's brain had atrophied to just 615 grams, about half of normal. Of course! Any part of the human body is subject to the rule of "use it or lose it." If you don't exercise your arm, it withers over time. The same principle applies to the brain.

In spite of this deprivation, the tiny flicker of life did not give up easily. The feeding tube came out for the last time on the afternoon of March 18, 2005; Terri fought on without food or even an ice chip for another thirteen days and nights. She at one point received a single drop of Communion wine on her tongue; when the monsignor returned another day to administer a second Communion, police had been ordered to turn him away. Yet Terri hung on longer than most experts predicted. Don't tell me she didn't have a will to live!

When the end finally came on March 31, I consoled myself with the thought that she was finally in the arms of Someone who would love her once again. She had been so deprived—not just in the last thirteen days, but for close to thirteen years. I had been rooting for her to hang on. Now I only slumped down on the bed and gave in to a giant sigh.

David—if I had dared inform him about all this—would have summed up the situation accurately: "Bad news," indeed.

"Perfect" or Nothing

Not long ago a friend asked me, "If you had been able to see ahead to all you have gone through to help David these past sixteen years, would it have been overwhelming?"

I answered, "After what the Schindler family had to endure, we are simply thankful we had the opportunity to care for and love David as we saw fit. She had a wonderful family who would have given anything to give her what we have been able to give David: a chance to get better at home in a loving environment!"

So what made the Terri Schiavo case so difficult for our society to decide? Why did we not automatically err on the side of life? Even today, whenever we face a body that has been mangled in some way, why do we so often hesitate before trying to restore it?

Disability is intimidating, I know. Our culture wants a perfect person. If somebody is profoundly imperfect, it makes the rest of the population a tad uncomfortable. They glance at the rolling eyes or the drool, and it gives them the creeps. They'd rather not watch.

Many school friends of our son simply could not handle a broken David; that's why they never came to visit. I suspect more than one person in Yakima has said, or at least thought, "Do the Nunleys still have that kid at their place? They ought to just face reality and put him in a home somewhere. Are they crazy or what?"

The drive for physical perfection is, if anything, getting stronger in our culture. The coin of the realm is outward beauty. "Extreme makeovers" are all the rage. More and more teen girls are asking for, and getting, a new kind of high school graduation gift: breast implants. They want to look "mature" when they go off to college in the fall.

On the male side, guys are equally concerned with physical prowess and demonstrating strength and agility; the rising tide is "extreme sports." Young men try to prove their value by what they can do with a skateboard, a bungee cord, a mountain bike. Applause and approval go to the most daring.

In the face of all this, I simply want to affirm that God sees no difference between the perfectly fit and the dreadfully disabled. David appears no less valuable in his eyes now than he was before the accident. God's love, grace, and compassion have stayed the same throughout all these years. He created my son's life in the first place, and he cherishes it to the present day. Cosmetics and profiles in the mirror are beside the point.

When, from a human perspective, you find yourself looking at a child who is now only one-third of what he or she used to be, you can throw up your hands and run—or you can get to work with the one-third that's left. Every time the person makes the tiniest step of progress, it is a precious moment. He picks up a glass for the first time, or she says a new word, or he signals that he needs to go to the bathroom—and you rejoice. You're making headway. You're building a future.

About 1.4 million Americans sustain a traumatic brain injury each year, most of them young people. Every one of these is devastating, spawning a flurry of difficult questions. Somewhere between ten and fifteen thousand of these sons and daughters are left in a "vegetative state." Shall we just give up and turn our attention instead to those who are whole in body and mind? No, a thousand times, no.

Families and friends play an especially crucial role in bringing back the severely damaged. Dr. Nancy Childs, a Texas neurologist who has studied many hospital treatment records, says of the brain-injured patient, "When you can barely do anything and it takes a tremendous effort to get that response out, you'll do it for someone who is recognizable versus someone who isn't."[10] The same is true in later stages of recovery. For all the limitations of us "amateurs," we have an undeniable advantage in getting through the fog to someone we love. No professionally trained stranger will ever match us in that arena.

In fact, not only Dale and I but our four other sons played a role in David's rehabilitation. Bringing David home required many sacrifices, especially from our two youngest, who were still at home. Bill was sixteen at the time, and Steve was just turning eight. Through it all, they both maintained high grades, received citizenship awards and college scholarships, and helped at home when needed. Their love for David made the sacrifices worth it as they saw him slowly but steadily improve.

They have both pursued careers in the medical field. Their experience with David has given them special empathy for people who are suffering and in need of help. Now thirty-two years old, Bill is an outstanding surgical nurse. We even hear from doctors about his caring touch with patients. He married his sweet wife, Libby, in 1995. She is director of the surgical program at Yakima Valley Community College. They have three adorable children.

Bill recently shared with me what he has learned from our family trials. "When something bad happens, you have two choices: the easy route, which is a pity party, depression, and spiraling downward, or the route of accepting what the Lord has allowed and, with his help, meeting the situation head-on."

Steve, now almost twenty-four, works at Creekside Physical Therapy and specializes in sports medicine. With the West Valley High School Sports Medicine Team, he went to the state level of competition all four years. He enjoyed playing football, wrestling, and pitching for the baseball team. Dozens of times we packed David up and took him to watch his brother's games. During Steve's junior year he was selected by his instructors to attend the Youth Leadership Forum on Medicine at Georgetown University. He also attended the International Youth Leadership Forum on Medicine in New Zealand and Australia the following year. He graduated from high school and is represented in the 2000–01 edition of *Who's Who*

Among American High School Students. In August 2005 he married the love of his life, Erin. She graduated from Central Washington University just before their wedding and works in promotions for the Seattle Seahawks.

In an ironic twist, we really had taken to heart all of Dr. Smith's warnings near the beginning about the total destruction of our marriage, our children becoming dropouts, the loss of all our friends, and our being woefully stuck alone with our "vegetable" son. We were determined to prove her wrong: You see, we had a strength in the Lord that she knew nothing about. In fact, the trial deepened us all.

I want to get to the end of my life and be able to say that I did everything I could for David. That I left no option unexplored. That I refused to quit. That I loved and worked and coaxed and prayed for him to be the best he could be, given the circumstances. Otherwise I could not face my Lord.

I look at David these days and see so much more than a "problem" to be managed. He is a fountain of constant happiness to all who know him. Peggy Latham, his case manager at the state office of aging and long-term care, was visiting with him one day when he lapsed into speaking in his high squeal, which happens often. I interjected my usual motherly correction, "David, use your low voice, okay? We like to hear your low voice."

"It's all right," Peggy said to me. "That's his *joy* coming through! I love to hear him so happy."

Life is a treasure given to us all. It doesn't have to be perfect to be valuable. How we handle it reflects our true character. We must treat life with honor, respect, and diligence, knowing that the Creator of life would have it no lesser way.

Ode to a Brother

This poem was composed by sixteen-year-old Bill McRae a few weeks after encountering the extent of his older brother's brain damage.

He was strong as an ox;
   He had a personality of his own,
      He never complained or groaned about anything—
      He just loved life altogether.

Always pulling jokes
   But helping the old folks;
      He was stubborn as a mule
         Things had to be his own way
            Till that tragic day.

A mess, you may say . . .
   but he wanted to ride a stupid motorcycle
   and "glide with the wind,"
      —sail like a bird—
         till that tragic day:

The bird broke its wing,
   The wind died down,
      The man who was almost perfect wrecked,
         He is still in the hospital three months later.
         He is waiting to come out of a coma.

He is so bad he can't even say mama,
   Whom he loved dearly, and so do I,
      He is so bad he can't . . .

go to the restroom
tie his own shoes
can't even sit up without someone holding him
or even brush his teeth.

All of this strongness, personality,
   Lovingness for life; the jokes,
      And helping the old folks
         Could all be taken away from him.

Why do I love this person so?
   This person is my brother.
      He made me who and what I am today,
         That is why I love him so.

And from now on I will be here for him every day.
I LOVE YOU, DAVE.

David McRae, 1987

"I am certain that God, who began the good work within you, will continue his work until it is finally finished on the day when Christ Jesus returns."

PHILIPPIANS 1:6, NLT

Afterword

by Derrick L. Hassert, PhD

Brain damage comes in many shapes and sizes, and its effects vary widely. Yet when it occurs, it often produces profound ethical questions about the nature of personhood. After trauma, stroke, or disease, is this human being still the same person he or she once was? Years ago, it is likely that the basic liberal humanist position would have been "Yes, of course—this is the same human being, having the same inherent worth and dignity as he or she did before the injury, and he or she should be treated accordingly."

However, many contemporary philosophers and bioethicists are now addressing this question—the question of personhood—in terms of interests, level of awareness, and the autobiographical abilities of the brain-damaged human. If one of these categories is found to be lacking to a certain degree, the designation of "person" might be stripped from the individual. This manner of thinking leads to other questions. How severe must the deficit be before the designation is taken away? What then are the legal rights of this "nonperson"? The answers to such questions are as numerous as the individuals producing the philosophies that bring them about.

Texts on clinical neuropsychology sometimes include a dedication of the volume to "the patients" based upon their cases providing evidence of the power of the "human spirit" to strive after triumph in the face of adversity.[11] Not only do cases of brain damage and recovery show us the power of the human will and spirit, neuroanatomical research on recovery from brain damage has also revealed the remarkable resilience of the human brain and its capacity to adapt in the face of trauma. This ability is usually referred to as "neuroplasticity." Knowledge of this concept is important in terms of making plans for neurological rehabilitation.

For recovery to occur, the person—and the nervous system of the person—needs to be challenged. The brain must be, in a very real sense, forced by environmental challenge to rewire itself. People may have to relearn names, faces, how to speak, how to walk, or even how to communicate using ways they probably had never imagined before the trauma. Brain damage and its effects exist on a continuum. Patients who have lingered in comas for several years have emerged unexpectedly, and nurses and physicians often comment that the continued presence and attempts at communication on the part of the families may have helped. Verbal and tactile stimulation were provided constantly, even in apparently hopeless situations.

While such examples are admittedly anecdotal, such efforts may have aided in the process of recovery. It is perhaps wise to lean toward optimism in these matters (although I know some may not agree). Better to provide the patient with environmental stimulation than to assume that no recovery is possible. Many patients with profound brain damage simply are given up on because they are given a diagnosis that places them in a hopeless category.

A British study conducted at the Royal Hospital for Neurodisability found that of the patients given a diagnosis of being in a "persistent vegetative state" (most clearly defined by an inability to engage in intentional behavior), 43 percent were

classified incorrectly as such, perhaps because not enough time
had been spent with the patients to ascertain whether they
could communicate.[12] Of course, if only a short block of time
is spent with a severely brain damaged patient and the clinician
is unlucky enough not to observe any attempts at communication during that period, the patient will be left without rehabilitation due to being considered a "lost cause." The dividing
line between hope and hopelessness, between the classification
of a persistent vegetative state and a state of minimal consciousness, is very slim indeed. Care should be taken before a
final label is applied to the patient.

Why this lengthy segue into neuroplasticity and the impor-
tance of proper, careful diagnosis? The traditional Christian
teaching concerning the nature of humanity rests in the
assumption that humans are created in the image of God, that
there is inherent dignity in this creature who is valued above
all other creatures. Classical Western humanism embraced this
view as well, even after uprooting the idea from a theistic
mooring. It is still the underpinning of our society and the
practice of medicine and the pursuits of biomedical research.

Often the concept of being created in the image and like-
ness of God has been unpacked in Jewish and Christian theology to mean that God is rational, creative, personal, and loving;
these characteristics are, to some degree, reflected in this creature made in his image.[13] Pope John Paul II, in his philosophi-
cal writings on Christian anthropology, argued that the most
important element expressed in the nature of the human being
is the ability to love and to be loved.[14]

Many clerics and clinicians have commented that when all
else is stripped from people through damage to the brain,

when rationality and creativity are cruelly taken away, one thing that comes through is their continued ability to give and respond to the love of other human beings. This isn't a very clinical or objective element to look for, and it doesn't fit well in philosophies that want to quantify interests or autobiographical capabilities and judge the value of human life accordingly. However, it is one that speaks to a true humanism that should (I would hope) strike a chord in the hearts of all people who seek to love and be loved as creatures carrying within them dignity and worth.

Derrick L. Hassert, PhD is an assistant professor of psychology at Trinity Christian College, Palos Heights, Illinois.

This article, "Still in the Image of God? The Ethical Challenge of Brain Damaged Persons," originally appeared on the Center for Bioethics and Human Dignity Web site (http://www.cbhd.org/resources/bioethics/hassert_2005-09-22.htm). Copyright © 2005. Used with permission.

Acknowledgments

Thank you to . . .

Bill Campbell, for his good humor and patience while helping me fix my computer messes; and to his wife, **Joy**, who helped me type much of the information until I learned to use a computer myself.

All the "patterners" who helped with David's rehabilitation—**Dwayne Taylor; Floyd** and **Cheryle Strauss**, our neighbors; **Steve Nunley; Richard** and **Jacquie Wonner; Bud** and **Judy Graves; Gene Kimmel**, who started our sessions with wonderful prayers, and his wife, **Erma; Millie Johnson**, a wonderful friend who has supported me many times when I desperately needed a friend; **Debbie Page; Joy Campbell; Pastor Dwight Hires** and **family; Leslie** and **Lois Robinson; Glen Laney; Paul Dressel III; Ron Jackson** and **family;** and **Lyle Holmes**.

Three teenage boys who were extraordinary in their commitment to pattern David all four years were **Todd Campbell**, now an airline captain with a major airline; **Dean Campbell**, an aeronautical engineer in Seattle; and **Brandt Urwin** (Debbie Page's son), who graduated with an electrical engineering degree. Brandt was an exceptional athlete with many awards, but when asked by our pastor, Rick Harpel, what his most meaningful award was, he said, "The Yakima City Council Volunteer Recognition for patterning David."

Dorothy Dyer and **Kathy Perrigo**, special friends and prayer partners.

Pastor Wayne Pickens, a loving shepherd, and his gracious wife, **Bonnie**; David will never forget Pastor Pickens's kindness and support.

Dr. Roger Bracchi and his wonderful wife, **Lori**, who came with their children, **Adam** and **Kara**, to pray and to visit David many times.

Dr. Marjorie Henderson, who has worked in the rehab unit at Yakima Regional Medical and Cardiac Center for more than ten years; she always does what she can to make life easier for families struggling with head injuries or other afflictions.

Dr. Michael Sean Mullin, who works with Dr. Henderson in the rehab unit; his introduction to treadmill therapy using a climbing harness was a breakthrough not only for David but also for other head-injury families who have come to see our setup.

Dr. T. W. Hill, the neurosurgeon who originally saved David's life; and **Dr. Christopher Moreno**, who brought David through many life-threatening moments at St. Joseph Regional Medical Center in Lewiston, Idaho.

The ICU nurses at St. Joseph, who gave David the very best care and kept us informed day and night in the critical first days; they carefully measured time intervals down to the second when they could safely administer the next dose of drugs to control his brain pressure.

Ron Finlay, past president of the Washington State Head Injury Association, and his wife, **Em**; together they provided such wonderful comfort to families dealing with head injury, having gone through this trauma themselves when their son, Ron Jr., was twelve.

Peggy Latham at the state office of aging and long-term care, who has helped us in every possible way to enable David to become as independent as possible; we owe her a multitude of thanks.

Michael Riker, a compassionate young man from our church who has taken David to movies, the park, and various other places; he really brightens David's day when he comes.

Dorothy Welk, my dear mother-in-law, who has always given me a shoulder to cry on when I needed one; God must have handpicked her for me.

Cara Anderson, an especially gifted nurse who personally went to bat for David.

Linda Sharp, who was God's gift to David at the scene of the accident.

A family in Ellensburg, Washington, **Paul** and **Marsha Cloutier**, who are giving their all to help their head-injured son, Ron.

Charlene Taylor, a single mom who also does a great job helping her son, Steve.

Walt and **Lois Funston**, my parents, who called every day for the first two years after David's accident; I am so thankful to them for teaching me what loyalty, love, honesty, faith, and hard work are all about, and I love them with all my heart.

Dale's two sons, **Skip** and **Randy Nunley** (and Randy's wife, **Karen**), whom the Lord sent to help us after David's accident.

Andre Cadousteau, David's caregiver. Without him or someone like him, our goal of getting David to live semi-independently would be impossible. He is a caregiver extraordinaire.

Countless people who have prayed, brought meals, and helped us cope; we can't possibly recall every name, but the Lord knows of your sacrifice for us. These are the body of Christ, his church. This book is a thankful tribute to the faithfulness of God and to each person who has helped David become a functional human being once again. They have all made "fighting for David" possible.

"And now these three remain: faith, hope and love. But the greatest of these is love" (1 Corinthians 13:13).

Endnotes

1 "Five Wishes" can be ordered from http://www.agingwithdignity.org/ 5wishes.html. Other helpful resources on end-of-life decision making include Gary P. Stewart et al., *Basic Questions on End of Life Decisions: How Do We Know What's Right?* (Grand Rapids: Kregel, 1998) and John F. Kilner, Arlene B. Miller, and Edmund D. Pellegrino, eds., *Dignity and Dying: A Christian Appraisal* (Grand Rapids: Eerdmans, 1996).

2 Cynthia L. Jones and Janis S. Lorman, *Traumatic Brain Injury: A Guide for the Patient and Family* (Stow, Ohio: Interactive Therapeutics, Inc., 1988).

3 Tony Semerad, "Answered Prayers," *Yakima Herald-Republic* (June 23, 1991).

4 Glenn Doman, *What to Do about Your Brain-Injured Child* (Wyndmoor, Penn.: Gentle Revolution Press, 2003).

5 Chandler Erossard, *Look* magazine (July 31, 1962), 60–66.

6 For more information on the Institutes for the Achievement of Human Potential, see http://www.iahp.org.

7 Mark Galli, "Questions for Both Sides," *Christianity Today* (May 2005), 58.

8 Mark Fuhrman, *Silent Witness* (New York: William Morrow, 2005), 245.

9 Judith Graham, "Signs of Consciousness," *Chicago Tribune* (July 31, 2005).

10 Ibid.

11 Jenni A. Ogden, *Fractured Minds: A Case-Study Approach to Clinical Neuropsychology* (New York: Oxford University Press, 1996); see also the dedication in Brenda Rapp, ed., *The Handbook of Cognitive Neuropsychology* (Philadelphia: Psychology Press, 2001).

12 Keith Andrews, Lesley Murphy, Ros Munday, and Clare Littlewood, "Misdiagnosis of the Vegetative State: Retrospective Study in a Rehabilitation Unit," *British Medical Journal* 313 (1996): 13–16.

13 See Moses Maimonides, *The Guide for the Perplexed* (New York: Barnes and Noble, 2004); Michael Pomazansky, *Orthodox Dogmatic Theology* (Platina, Calif.: Saint Herman Press, 1994).

14 Andrew Woznicki, *A Christian Humanism: Karol Wojtyla's Existential Personalism* (New Britain, Conn.: Mariel, 1980).

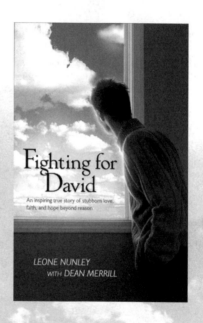